BEYOND AGE RAGE

Also by David Cravit

THE NEW OLD:
How the Boomers Are
Changing Everything ... Again

www.davidcravit.com

BEYOND AGE RAGE

How the Boomers and Seniors Are Solving the War of the Generations

DAVID CRAVIT

BPS books

Toronto and New York

Copyright © 2012 by David Cravit

All rights reserved. No part of this publication may be reproduced or transmitted in any form or by any means, electronic or mechanical, including photocopying, recording, or any information storage and retrieval system, without permission in writing from the publisher.

Published in 2012 by
BPS Books
Toronto & New York
www.bpsbooks.com
A division of Bastian Publishing Services Ltd.
www.bastianpubserv.com

ISBN 978-1-926645-95-7

Cataloguing-in-Publication data available from
Library and Archives Canada.

Cover: Gnibel
Author photograph: John Burridge
Text design and typesetting: Daniel Crack, KD Books
   www.kdbooks.ca

Printed by Lightning Source, Tennessee. Lightning Source paper, as used in this book, does not come from endangered old-growth forests or forests of exceptional conservation value. It is acid free, lignin free, and meets all ANSI standards for archival-quality paper. The print-on-demand process used to produce this book protects the environment by printing only the number of copies that are purchased.

To Cynthia,
with love and
gratitude

Contents

Preface ix
Acknowledgments xi
A Note on Generational Terminology xiii

1 BATTLE STATIONS
1 – This Time, It's Different 3
2 – The Converging Causes 9

2 THE COMPETING ARMIES
3 – Boomers and Seniors: Firepower 27
4 – Boomers and Seniors: Attitudes 35
5 – Boomers and Seniors: Objectives 46
6 – Millennials: The Kids Are Not All Right 58

3 AGE RAGE – AND BEYOND
Chapter 7 – The Jobs Battle 83
Chapter 8 – The Political Battle 120
Chapter 9 – Generational Effectiveness:
    A Case Study 143
Chapter 10 – The Boomers Take Action 166

Conclusion 195
A Note on Sources 199
Index 203

Preface

My first book, *The New Old*, published in October 2008, described the many ways boomers were reinventing aging, some of the immediate consequences that could be expected, and how organizations could respond.

The book generated a lot of interest. I was fortunate enough to be asked to speak at a number of events; I did many radio call-ins, was interviewed in newspapers and magazines, and conducted some podcasts. I'd like to think this flurry of activity was the result of my brilliant writing, but the truth is, it was hard to miss with such a topic. The idea that aging could actually be reinvented was inherently compelling: Just imagine, a single generation could overthrow the established attitudes and expected behaviors of centuries. Automatically retire at 65? Not on your life. Stop having sex? Never! Shuffle off the stage quietly? No chance. I had a tremendous inventory of real-life examples to present and solid grounds for the strategic and tactical recommendations I was making to organizations that wanted to communicate more effectively with "the new old."

Although there was a chapter on politics, the book focused on individual behavior – what boomers were thinking and doing about health, money, sex, work, and retirement. While it described changes that were bound to have profound longer-term implications, most of the material (and the recommendations) dealt with the here and now.

Even as I was writing *The New Old*, however, I was starting to think about those longer-term implications. Then came the economic meltdown – within a month or two of the book's publication – and suddenly those implications were more immediate. The reinvention of aging and the emergence of the new old was no longer just an interesting social or cultural phenomenon; it was setting into motion a whole chain reaction of challenges to the way our society operates, the resources it commands and how it allocates them, and what it expects at different points along the human life span. The new old, I saw, was quickly giving rise to "the new young" – and the new adult, the new workplace, the new family, the new everything.

Hence this book. It is my effort to track the early moves in what will be an entire reordering of our world as a consequence of the reinvention of aging. These early moves are, as we will see, accompanied by a large amount of noise and acrimony – thus Age Rage, an apparent war between the generations. My goal is to show how and why this is happening, what's real and what's myth, and where it all may lead.

Although I have tried to use a maximum of evidence and a minimum of personal opinion, it is impossible to avoid being selective concerning the facts presented and the lines of argument adopted. However, I am confident that even if you disagree with some of the positions I have taken, you will share my conviction that the conflict we see between the generations is actually the harbinger of a radically different – and necessarily different – society of the future. You may also be surprised to learn that it is the older generations – the boomers and seniors – who are driving the reforms.

Acknowledgments

I have a number of people to thank for their assistance with this project.

I am indebted to Moses Znaimer, Brent Green, and Luanne Whitmarsh for taking time to review the manuscript and for the generosity of their comments. I particularly appreciate Moses Znaimer's encouragement to dig deeper into the material and find the really important stories behind the more lurid Age Rage headlines.

I am indebted to my colleagues at ZoomerMedia for continuing to give me a front-row seat on the revolution in aging. I particularly want to acknowledge Ross Mayot, with whom I have had many lively discussions and debates on some of the issues explored here; he has kept me on my toes and (he doesn't know this) has been an important unseen critic against whose standards I have tried to measure the positions I advance here and how I present them. I also want to acknowledge the considerable help of Leanne Wright, who contributed valuable thinking on how the book could best be positioned and promoted.

I am grateful for the cooperation of Bill Meloche, Ken Coates, Anya Kamenetz, Michael Morris, and Christina Newberry, who all consented to e-mail interviews so I could incorporate their important knowledge and insights on the issue.

Brent Green, who has been a very important influence on my thinking, not only reviewed the manuscript but also consented to an e-mail interview. Brent understands the boomer generation. He is a very innovative thinker on the topic of marketing to boomers, and I have benefited from his wisdom, encouragement, and friendship.

I thank Don Bastian, who was first my agent and is now my publisher, for his unfailing enthusiasm for the project. Don helped me to focus and frame the entire book and to find deeper layers of content. He has high standards, yet is easy to work with – a rare combination!

I thank my family – my wife, Cynthia, and our children Rachel, Nathaniel, and Nicholas – for their patience and good humor in putting up with a writer who requires so much quiet in the house. To all of you I say: I could not have undertaken, let alone completed, a project like this without your help and support.

Finally, I must emphasize that although I have drawn on the knowledge and ideas of many people in writing *Beyond Age Rage*, any errors are entirely my responsibility.

A Note on Generational Terminology

THROUGHOUT this book I present the views and behaviors of boomers, seniors, Gen Xers, and millennials. For the reader's convenience, the following indicates how I define these generational terms.

Boomers, or baby boomers, refers to the generation born immediately after World War II – "boom" because there was a dramatic increase in the birth rate in North America, the UK, and Australia. Demographers do not agree on the precise starting date and ending date of the baby boom. Some demographers include babies who were conceived when soldiers came home during leave – hence their baby boom starts as early as 1943. The boom did not unfold evenly in all countries, either. In the UK, for example, there was big growth in 1946, 1947, and 1948, followed by a drop, then another surge in the early 1960s.

The consensus seems to be that the boom spans, roughly, the period from 1946 to 1965. Using that benchmark, the youngest boomer today, in 2012, is 47 years of age, and the oldest is 66. We can give or take a year or so on either side; none of the arguments in this book depend on a more precise agreement.

Seniors is a term generally used to describe people who

have reached the age of 65, which is the traditional or expected year of retirement. The term, therefore, is not confined to those born in a particular birth range – everyone is eventually going to be a senior. The oldest baby boomers are now, therefore, seniors. In this book, I frequently use "boomers and seniors" to describe a single "army" in the war of the generations. When I use actual numbers, I have been careful not to double-count the boomers.

The parents of the boomers are a distinct generation of their own, and they have often been referred to as **the Greatest Generation** – in contrast to their heavily criticized boomer children. The term was first used by journalist Tom Brokaw as the title of a book about the generation that suffered through the Depression and then went on to fight World War II.

Generation X, or Gen Xers, is used to name the first generation born after the baby boom ended. The consensus date range is the early 1960s to about 1980 or 1981. The majority of Gen Xers have baby boomers as their parents, although the very oldest Gen Xers were born to the younger members of the Greatest Generation, and they would have had baby boomers as older siblings.

Millennials, or Generation Y, signifies the generation immediately following Generation X. They are also sometimes referred to as Generation Next or Echo Boomers. The consensus date range is from the early 1980s through to the late 1990s, although some demographers have pushed the definition as far as 2000 or 2001. The oldest millennials are approaching 30, and the youngest are in their early to mid-teens. For the purposes of my Age Rage thesis, I focus largely on those who are entering the workforce, have completed post-secondary education, or are still enrolled in post-secondary education.

Battle Stations

This Time, It's Different

"*THE* children now love luxury," the old man complained. "They have bad manners, contempt for authority; they show disrespect for elders and love chatter in place of exercise. Children are now tyrants, not the servants of their households. They no longer rise when elders enter the room. They contradict their parents, chatter before company, gobble up dainties at the table, cross their legs, and tyrannize their teachers."

Sound familiar?

The old man was Socrates.

He wasn't the first, or the last, to voice these sentiments. We could fill an entire volume with quotes of older people moaning about "the youth."

Writing about 300 years before Socrates, the historian Hesiod said, "I see no hope for the future of our people if they are dependent on the frivolous youth of today, for certainly all youth are reckless beyond words. When I was a boy, we were taught to be discreet and respectful of elders, but the present youth are exceedingly wise and impatient of restraint."

That was in 700 B.C.

Pick any time and you can find the same thing. Jonathan Swift in the 17th century: "No wise man ever wished to be younger." Oscar Wilde in the 19th: "I am not young enough to know everything." Evelyn Waugh in the 20th: "What is youth except a man or a woman before it is ready or fit to be seen?" Always the older folks dissing the kids. Codgers against teens, curmudgeons against whippersnappers. It's the way life works. You get older, you get grumpier. And "the kids" look less worthy of respect. "When I was your age ..." is a sentiment that we have been voicing since we first emerged from the caves.

So what's different now? What do I mean by the war of the generations? Is it really happening? Why is it worth a whole book? And why should you pay attention?

The answer starts with a single word – *longevity*.

In the past, it didn't really matter if the old folks thought the kids weren't up to snuff. In fact, it didn't even matter if they were right. The old folks were on their way out; they had little or no time left to do anything about their grievances. True, depending on the culture, there may have been a few ritualistic nods to their wisdom and experience, but in most cases they were complaining into the void – the power had already shifted to the younger generations. If you had to listen to Gramps fulminate against the kids, you might be amused, you might be annoyed, you might be bored ... but you certainly wouldn't be afraid. Gramps was in no position to do anything about his beefs.

This time it's different.

This time Gramps has plenty of time to do something. In North America, a healthy 60-year-old has at least a 50% chance of reaching 90, and that threshold is being pushed higher every year. In 1950, there were fewer than 3,000 centenarians in the world; today the number approaches half a million. And according to a 2009 report by the US National Institute of Aging, this number will jump to six million – no, that's not a typo, *six million centenarians* – by 2050.

In fact, I may be understating the trend. Scientists are talking – with perfectly straight faces – about being able to extend the human life span to 150, 200, or even more.

As a result, the age balance of our society is tilting steadily toward the older age groups. In both Canada and the USA, there are more people over the age of 60 than the total of high school and college students. This has never happened before. And the 45-plus population is the only group projected to increase as a percentage of the total population; the younger age groups will continue to represent smaller pieces of the pie.

What's more, as I demonstrated in my book *The New Old*, it isn't just that there are more old people than ever before. More importantly, they're not the *same* old people.

The baby boomers are completely reinventing the process of aging and the meaning of old. Whether it's shopping or travel or even sex, they are behaving much younger than any previous generation of the same age. They perceive themselves to have plenty of time left, and they are determined to get the most out of life for as long as they can. They are not retiring on schedule, in part because they don't want to, in part because they can't afford to.

The 45-plus age group (which Canadian media mogul Moses Znaimer has brilliantly relabeled "Zoomers") not only is very aware of its clout, but, given all those extra years of life span, is also determined not to surrender its domination.

This is particularly important at the ballot box. In both Canada and the USA, the 45-plus population accounts for about 60% of all votes cast in federal elections. Political parties have been amazingly slow to realize this; the media and their political pundits have, if anything, been even slower. But the recognition is starting to grow: The vaunted "youth vote" isn't big enough to be decisive. Going forward, it will be Gramps' agenda that carries the day.

Socrates died at 70. Today, unless of course he made the mistake again of impiety and poisoning the minds of the youth, he'd still be working – or attending a seminar on how to reinvent himself in a new career. And he'd be laughing at those disrespectful kids, not tut-tutting them, because he'd know that he and his buddies still had, nothing serious, a few decades left in which to see that their needs, wants, and values drive the agenda of society.

I'll be developing this case in more detail in the coming chapters. For those who want statistics, I'll provide them. But you probably already perceive that the population is indeed aging and today's old folks are acting a lot younger. You may even perceive, without further proof, that this will lead to some profound shakeups in the structure and operation of our society.

Okay – but *war*? Old *against* young? Surely I'm over-reaching here.

Of course, I'm not talking about an actual shooting war. But otherwise, does the metaphor hold up?

Generational warfare is definitely becoming an established shortcut for the media – which bang on about the selfish, greedy older generations engineering a war against the young. There are so many examples of this kind of language that it's almost a cliché.

And the emotional side effect – Age Rage – is certainly real enough. There is a tremendous amount of intergenerational rancor flying about, and you will see many examples in the pages that follow.

Most importantly, there are indeed some natural, and substantive, conflicts between the needs and wants of the boomers and seniors on the one hand, and those of the younger generations, particularly the millennials, on the other. The conflicts are made more intense by the simple fact of timing: The extended life span and feistier behavior of boomers and seniors are taking center stage precisely when the finances of Western economies, to put it mildly, are coming under extreme pressure. There isn't enough money to pay for all the commitments – to education, to health care, to pensions and retirement. Scarcity promotes a battle for the spoils; it's that simple.

In the chapters that follow, I will describe in more detail how these conflicts are being played out. I'll also present what may be a controversial thesis, that it is the *younger* people, not the older, who are at a disadvantage – specifically, the millennials, born between 1982 and 2001.

The millennials are competing for public funding (education), and, as we will see, are under great pressure in the job market, some of it from boomers who are not retiring on schedule. The millennials are significantly outnumbered, and they also have gone through a social and educational system (created largely by the boomers) that has left them seriously ill-equipped to deal with the challenges they will face.

If we adopt the imagery of the headlines and see the boomers and seniors as one army and the millennials as the other, it is, perhaps surprisingly, the younger forces who are ill-equipped for the struggle.

They know it, too. Their frustrations are already starting to build. Age Rage is certainly no myth.

For simplicity of presentation – and to avoid bogging you down with repeated disclaimers all the way along – I am going to start by adopting the war analogy. We'll look at the intergenerational conflicts – for jobs, for public funds, for political power – as if they really were battles between competing armies.

But then comes the twist.

Unlike any other war, in this one the winning army is actively helping the losing forces, even as the conflict is still unfolding. Even as they continue to reinvent aging and wage a very aggressive (and successful) campaign to protect their needs and wants, the boomers and seniors are at the same time fighting for the other side. They are launching a Marshall Plan for the benefit of the millennials. The plan goes beyond writing a few checks. As we will see, it foreshadows what will be an amazingly dynamic and creative reshaping of our entire society.

The war of the generations looks and sounds like a war because it's taking place against a background of upheaval and uncertainty, a time when *all* trade-offs, not just intergenerational ones, can seem to be life-or-death zero-sum decisions.

But we should not be so caught up in the war imagery that we overlook the important and creative solutions that are emerging. If Age Rage, by its very intensity, provokes us to think more deeply about the longer-term implications of longevity and the reinvention of aging, then it can have a healthy effect. But the real benefit comes only when we go beyond Age Rage, to more quickly identify, and study, the new ideas and forces that are already starting to turn the unstoppable reinvention of aging into something dynamic, creative, and of enduring value.

Going beyond Age Rage matters to a number of important players in society – politicians and policymakers, educators, marketers, and those who deliver health and social services. It should also matter to the protagonists themselves. I hope this book will provoke some fresh thinking for all of them, and others.

The Converging Causes

GREATER longevity – all by itself – would be bound to produce serious new changes in the makeup and operation of society. Even if the economy were roaring, if we were drowning in money and other resources, we would still need to make dramatic adjustments because of the presence of so many more people living past all previous definitions of "old."

Age Rage implies that we're not talking about orderly adjustments. We're not talking about methodical, long-term plans arrived at through polite and constructive consultation. Rage means intensity. Rage means fear – maybe even loss of control.

Such a menacing condition can't be the product of one cause alone – and especially a cause that is working its power gradually, as longevity has done. No, rage is the result of several causes that are coming together at the same time. A perfect storm turning what could have been a manageable adjustment of competing interests into what appears to be an intense and bitter war.

What are these causes? I have identified five.

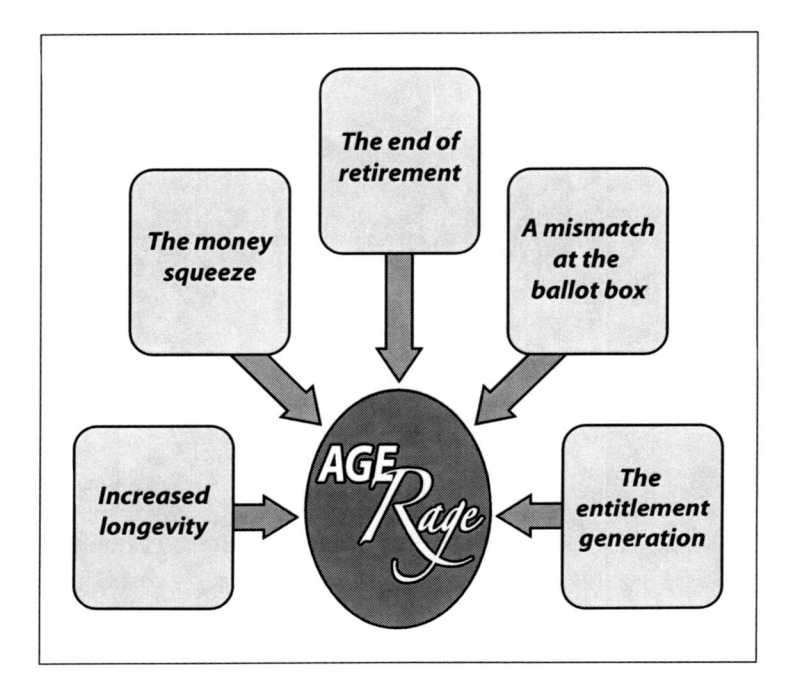

```
              ┌──────────────┐
              │ The end of   │
              │ retirement   │
              └──────────────┘
┌──────────┐                    ┌──────────┐
│The money │                    │A mismatch│
│ squeeze  │                    │  at the  │
│          │                    │ballot box│
└──────────┘                    └──────────┘
              ╲      │      ╱
               ╲     ▼     ╱
                ( AGE RAGE )
               ╱           ╲
┌──────────┐                    ┌──────────┐
│Increased │                    │   The    │
│longevity │                    │entitlement│
│          │                    │generation│
└──────────┘                    └──────────┘
```

Cause #1 – Increased Longevity

There are actually two components to longevity:

- Without any change in the "normal" maximum human life span of about 100, more and more people are living longer

- The life span itself *is* being extended; many serious scientists argue that it could easily reach 125, 150, or even higher

Taken together, these two realities permanently shift the demographic balance of our society. The numbers are unassailable.

First, here's the picture of how much longer people are living. The chart, based on the findings of Statistics Canada, shows life expectancy at birth, in Canada, from 1921 to the present.

Life Expectancy in Canada*

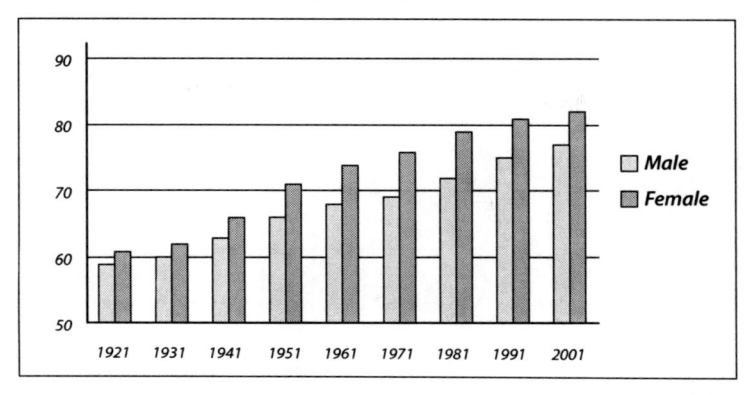

[Bar chart showing Male and Female life expectancy in Canada from 1921 to 2001, with values rising from around 58-60 years in 1921 to approximately 77-82 years in 2001.]

While life expectancy in the USA is slightly lower, the trend line is very similar.

But life expectancy at birth tells only part of the story. Average life expectancy is pulled down, of course, by people who die in infancy, childhood, or younger adulthood. What's your outlook if you manage to reach the age of 65?

In 1900, the average North American male who had managed to reach age 65 could look forward to about 11 more years of life. For women, it was about 12 more years. Over the next 40 years, the number hardly budged. In 1940, 65-year-old men could expect to live another 12 years, while women could look forward to approximately 13.

But since World War II, thanks to dramatic advances in medical and drug therapies, plus more knowledge about diet, prevention, and healthier living (not smoking, for example), those numbers have increased sharply. Today the average 65-year-old male is looking at almost 20 years more; the average woman, 21 years.

As a consequence, the demographic dominance in our society now lies with the older age groups. And we're just getting started.

---

* Further information on the sources of charts throughout this book may be found in "A Note on Sources," pages 199-201.

Here's the Canadian population pyramid, as projected by Statistics Canada. The chart shows the number of people in each age group.

Canadian Population Pyramids

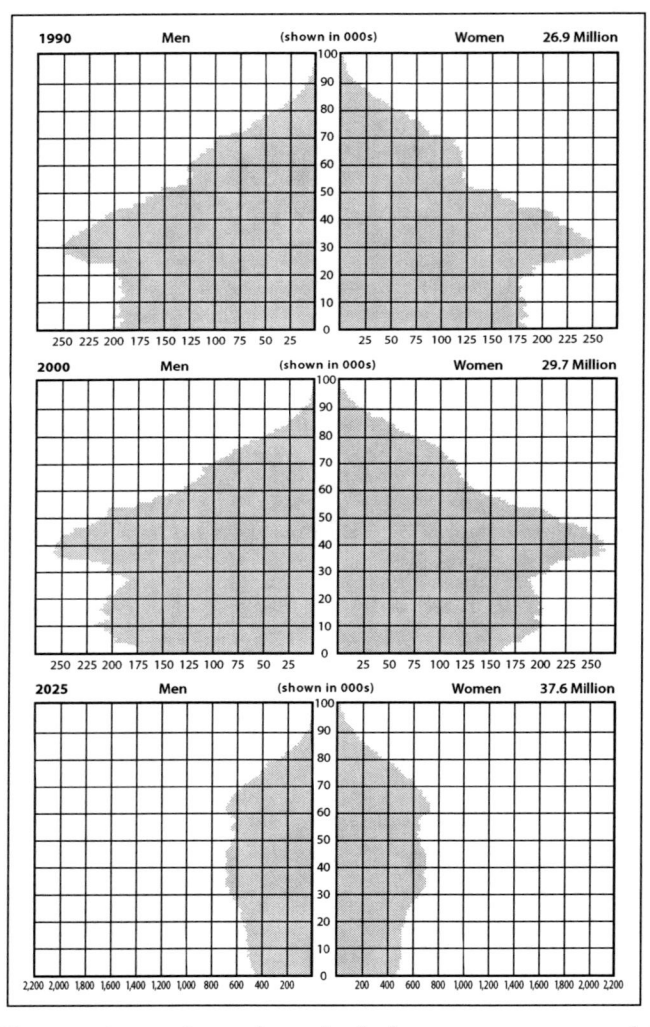

| 1990 | Men | (shown in 000s) | Women | 26.9 Million |

| 2000 | Men | (shown in 000s) | Women | 29.7 Million |

| 2025 | Men | (shown in 000s) | Women | 37.6 Million |

You can instantly see how the bulge moves up, toward the older age groups.

The US numbers, from the US Census Bureau, are for slightly different years, but you can see the trend is the same. As the years go by, the number of people in the older age groups increases.

USA Population Pyramids

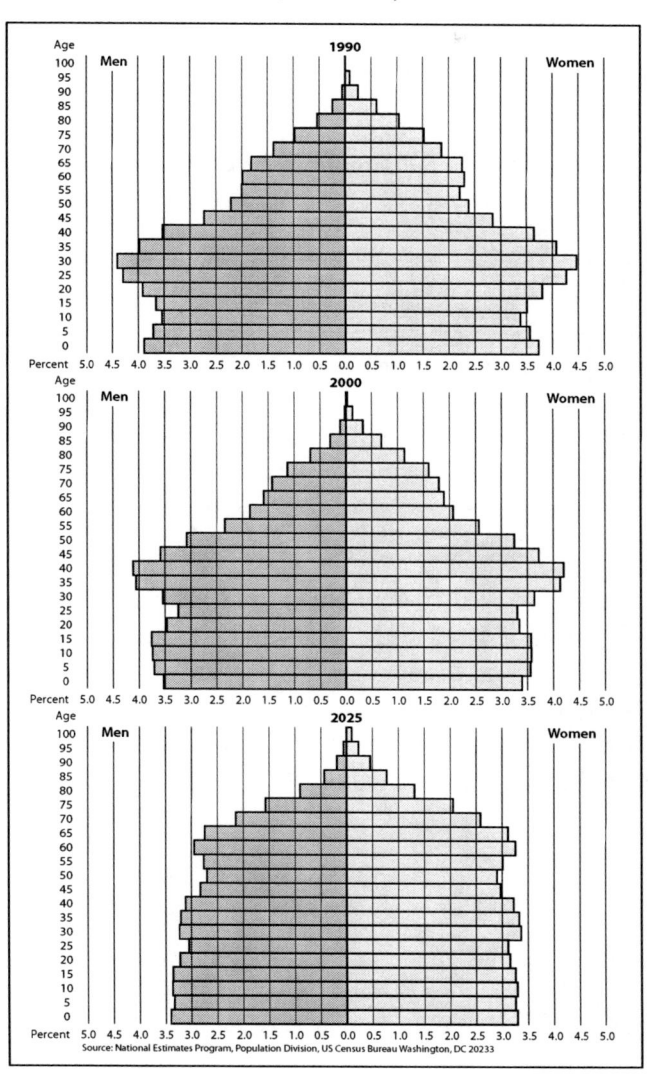

Source: National Estimates Program, Population Division, US Census Bureau Washington, DC 20233

THE CONVERGING CAUSES

These charts show the absolute numbers of people at each age break. But the real impact, especially in the context of a battle for control, is better illustrated by focusing on the adult population (18-plus) and expressing the numbers as a percentage of the total adult population. I've grouped boomers and seniors together as 45-plus. The picture, based on reports from Statistics Canada and the US Census Bureau, is dramatic and unambiguous.

First, the Canadian projection.

Canadian Adult Sub Groups by Percentage of Population

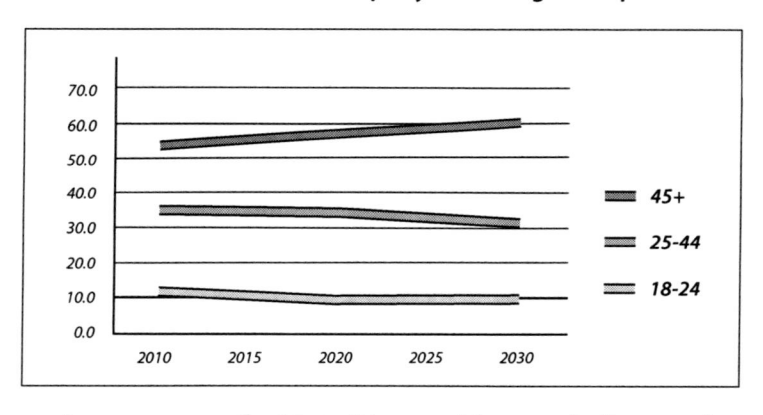

As you can see, the 18- to 24-year-old group declines gradually to just under 10% of the total adult population. The 25- to 44-year-old group drops from the low 30s to just above 30%, while the 45-plus group climbs from the low 50s to 60%.

Now the picture in the USA. As you can see, it's almost exactly the same as in Canada.

USA Adult Sub Groups by Percentage of Population

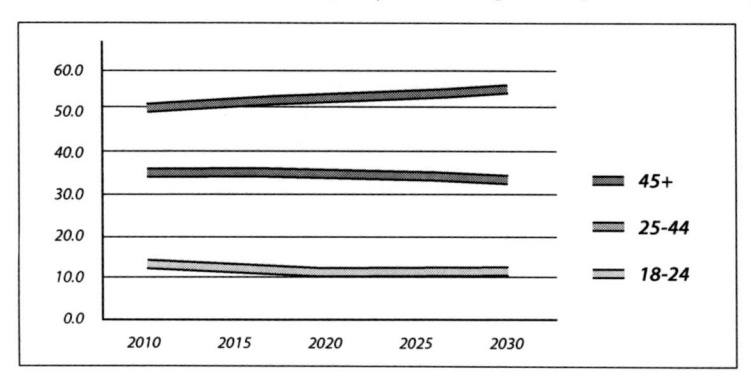

[Chart showing three lines from 2010 to 2030: 45+ rising from ~50 to ~55; 25-44 declining slightly from ~32 to ~30; 18-24 declining slightly from ~13 to ~11]

I realize you may be thinking, "Very clever, Cravit, but to create this numerical mismatch you've had to combine the groups of 45- to 64-year-olds and 65-plus. You've amalgamated an age span of four or five decades and stacked it up against a span of only 10 years (15 to 24). Is that fair?"

Answer: It doesn't need to be fair. It just needs to be accurate. There are two armies, and one is much bigger than the other (and will continue to grow). That's just the way it is.

"Not so fast," you come back. "What entitles you to believe all people 45-plus have the same interests, needs, and wants?"

Answer: They don't. In Canada, 45-plus means 15 million people, and in the USA 122 million people. So of course there is great diversity, in age, state of health, income, and tastes, as well as in social and political leanings. But my case doesn't depend on members of these groups being exactly the same any more than an army requires all of its soldiers to have identical characteristics. What unites an army is an overarching cause, a cause that trumps individual differences. And in this case, we have one – the money squeeze that is putting unbearable pressure on jobs, pensions, and social services *at exactly the same time* that increased longevity is demanding more of those resources.

Cause #2 – The Money Squeeze

I use the word "squeeze" very deliberately. It isn't just a matter of our running out of money to pay for the services and entitlements we've built into society. It's that we're running out of the money *precisely when* – thanks to aging – we need more of those services and entitlements.

I don't need to present pages and pages of evidence about the current financial crisis. Headlines in the traditional and Internet media tell us every day how our entire postwar model (much of which has been funded by public debt) is crashing and burning.

In Europe, sovereign debt crises in Greece, Spain, Italy, Portugal – and maybe more – are washing away the assumptions that have governed what society can provide by way of education, health care, welfare, pensions, and other benefits.

In the USA, the Social Security system now pays out more than it takes in and, if no reforms are made, will implode within 20 years. Total federal public debt in 2011 approached $14 trillion, an increase of 132% over the course of the preceding decade. That's without counting over $100 trillion in off-the-books future entitlement commitments (an accounting dodge that would land CEOs in jail if it were conducted in the private sector). And let's not forget over $1 trillion in *unfunded* state and local pension commitments.

In Canada, government finances are in relatively better shape, although governments at all levels are talking about the need to rein in spending. This is particularly true of the provinces: In many of them, spending has outpaced economic growth over the past decade, leading to serious deficits and the need for dramatic cutbacks.

This isn't a book about economics, and I am not a stock market forecaster. I don't intend to predict when and how all this will play out. It's a safe bet, though, that we are in for many years of belt-tightening; the only question is how orderly (in North America) or messy (in Europe) the process will be.

If it were just a matter of dollars, a younger demographic mix would possibly help our societies weather the storm. Even if our university graduates and youngest workers spent a whole decade trapped in menial jobs (or no jobs) and they didn't begin to get back on their feet again until, let's say, 2020, they would still have decades upon decades in which to rebuild their finances. They may look back on the early years of the 21st century the way the parents and grandparents of the boomers looked back on the Great Depression; the point is they still have plenty of time to recover.

But the demographic mix is not younger. Just for fun, I have compared the age mix of society during the Great Depression with today's. Here's the Canadian picture, comparing 1931 and 2011. The chart shows what percentage of the adult population (18 years and older) fell into the various age groups then and now.

Percentage of Canadian Age Groups During Depression and Now

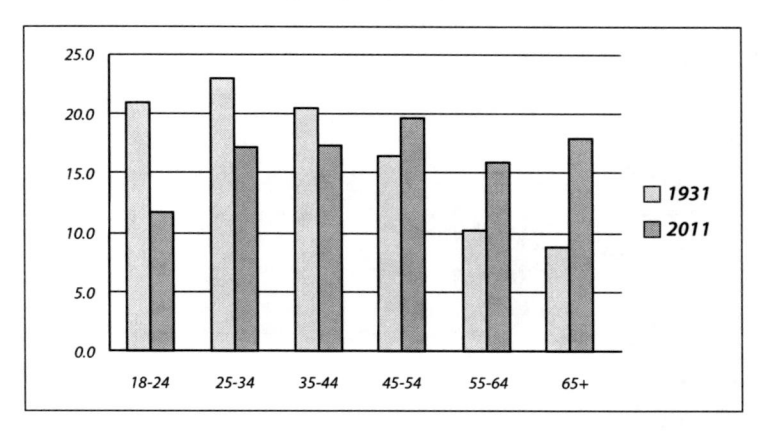

Bar chart showing percentages for age groups 18-24, 25-34, 35-44, 45-54, 55-64, 65+ comparing 1931 and 2011.

The 2011 numbers are no surprise, given the population pyramids and other data presented above. But look at 1931. Only one-third of the adult population was above the age of 45, which means that two-thirds of the adult population had anywhere from 25 to 50 years to go, based on life expectancy figures of that era. They had more than enough time to recover, at least to some degree, from the economic disaster.

I'm not saying they were happy about suffering through the Depression, or easygoing about the politicians who had failed them. (In Canada, the Liberals were able to successfully run for decades against the memory of Conservative R. B. Bennett, who had been in power at the start of the Depression; in the USA, the Democrats did the same with the memory of Herbert Hoover.) But for a substantial majority of the adult population, there were enough years left for them to bounce back.

Today, however, the percentage of adults over the age of 45 is 50% higher than it was in during the Great Depression. The percentage over the age of 65 is *double* what it was in 1931. The percentage of people with fewer years left to go is actually *greater* than the percentage with more years left to go. Here's the picture, again using Canadian numbers.

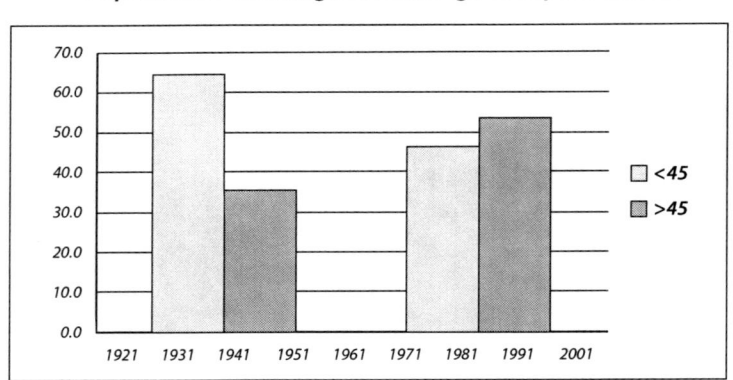

Population Percentage of Adult Age Groups in Canada

Crudely put, the "die sooner" population is now *larger* than the "die later" population – and the spread will only keep increasing.

This has never happened before in our history. And it places the money crunch in a very different light.

If worse comes to worst, the younger cohorts can more easily cut back, work for less, travel out of necessity to where the jobs are, somehow make do. Not only are they physically better able to adapt, but also, as I've pointed out with reference to the Great Depression, they have more years left in which to recoup their losses. But the older cohorts have no such slack. In fact, they require even more funding the longer they live.

And now they're the majority – that's the whole point. They have the strongest possible motive to grab (or not let go of) the biggest possible share of society's dwindling financial resources: Their lives depend on it.

One of most important areas where they are hanging on is the workplace.

Cause #3 – The End of Retirement

The boomers are not retiring on schedule. And even many seniors, who thought their retirement was secure, are being pushed back into the workforce.

For the boomers, it's a function of both need and attitude.

The "need" part is obvious. The boomers, as a generation, are seriously underfunded. Even without the crisis in the economy, they don't have enough money, in terms of pensions or other retirement savings, to comfortably carry them into their 90s or beyond. They need to keep generating more income. Retiring at age 65 is less and less possible.

The attitude part comes in … well, because they're the boomers, the Me Generation, after all. The generation whose needs, wants, and drives dominated society at every stage of their lives, whether they were kids or teens or young adults or 30-somethings. Why would they suddenly take a back seat now?

Not surprisingly, as I demonstrated in my book *The New Old*, the boomers are reinventing aging. They act much younger than people of the same age in any previous generation. They are absolutely unwilling to give up their power in the marketplace. They see work (whether for financial, social, or intellectual motives) as an essential component of self-validation.

Now throw in the recent stock market and real estate meltdown, and suddenly it's not just the boomers who are in trouble. Their parents – the seniors, who thought they were all set – now face economic calamity, too. Many of them are even being forced – suddenly and unexpectedly – into looking for a job. Often they are competing with the millennials. Even if the old-timers lose most of the face-offs, their collective presence in the market of job seekers can increase employer leverage and put downward pressure on wages. As if the millennials didn't already have enough problems, as we will see.

Because so many boomers and seniors are not moving out of the way when they're "supposed to," the jobs pipeline is blocked, making for a more difficult work passage for the generations behind them. Especially for the millennials, who are not exactly suffering in silence.

But the job market is only one front in the battle for scarce dollars. There is also the huge and complex network of public programs – pensions, health care, income supplements, and other social entitlements. It is vitally important to boomers and seniors that their piece of this action be protected (or even better, *increased*). Which takes us to another front in the looming war – the political arena.

Cause #4 – A Mismatch at the Ballot Box

The 45-plus population completely dominates at the ballot box. Not only is it larger than the millennial cohort to begin with, but it also turns out to vote in much greater numbers. In fact, in the average Canadian and American federal election, the combination of boomers and seniors casts *more than five times as many votes* as the millennials.

But do the boomers and seniors all vote the same way?

In good times, possibly not (although there is strong evidence that as people age they become more small-c conservative). But when governments are strapped for cash, as is certainly the case today, boomers and seniors can – and will

– coalesce to protect their benefits and entitlements. They can – and will – punish any politicians perceived to threaten those benefits and entitlements. Cutbacks, if they are needed, will be pushed onto the shoulders of younger generations.

Remember, too, that a significant number of baby boomers have parents who are still living. Even if the boomers are not yet worried, for themselves, about deficiencies in the healthcare system or the unsustainability of government pension plans, they are certainly being jolted into a heightened awareness of the threats faced by their parents. They are being forced, in a way, to anticipate old age, and all its vulnerability, by what they see happening to their own parents. So even if their own lifestyles are younger – which is certainly true – they must confront the shakiness of services and benefits that their parents have been counting on (and that most boomers are in no position to fund if government resources fall through).

This creates a powerful commonality of interests between the boomers and the seniors at the expense of the millennials, who certainly don't have the electoral muscle to protect their own interests.

Not that the millennials have a lot of muscle, period.

Cause #5 – The Entitlement Generation

In North America, absent massive immigration, it is a mathematical certainty that, as more people live longer, the older generations will out-populate the younger generations.

It is not my thesis, however, that the younger generations must necessarily be outgunned by older generations in a battle for resources. They might make up for their numerical disadvantage in other ways – being tougher, more aggressive, harder working, more innovative. There is no *a priori* reason why they should be unsuccessful.

The millennials specifically, however, are another matter. It is my thesis that they will lose the war to the boomers and seniors – and not just because of the cumulative power of the first four causes that we have examined (although that power is indeed formidable), but also because of huge deficiencies in their attitudes and capabilities as a group.

You may think that my use of the word "attitudes" implies some kind of moral condemnation, an attack on the millennials' values, on their worth as individuals. Let me be clear that I am talking only about their *fitness for struggle* – about their ability, as a generation, to take on the boomers and seniors. And in doing so, I am generalizing. Of course there are individuals in the millennial generation who do not fit the negative patterns I will describe. Thousands of them. Tens of thousands. (I am the proud father of millennials who definitely do not fit the mold.) But I bring plenty of evidence to support my claim that the millennials, as a group, are unfocused, non-ambitious, and have a sense of entitlement that is divorced from reality.

All of which makes them a very weak army – easy pickings for the boomers and seniors.

Let's recap.

Five forces are exerting their influence at the same moment:

An increase in longevity, causing an increase
in demand for age-related resources …

↓

… just when those resources are dwindling,
due to the economic meltdown …

↓

… thus driving more and more boomers
and seniors to defer retirement
(which the boomers are happy to do anyway, as
part of how they are reinventing aging) …

↓

… and also driving those boomers and
seniors to join forces at the ballot box,
to protect their threatened benefits and entitlements …

↓
… at risk to the millennials, who are too dysfunctional to do anything about it anyway, except get very mad

That's the big picture. Now let's drill down into some of the details.

The Competing Armies

FOR 40s 50s 60s 70s 80s PLUS

ZOOMER

MEDIA KIT 2012

Boomers and Seniors: Firepower

Do these people look old to you? Helpless? Ready to pack it in any time soon?

This is the cover shot of the 2012 media kit for *ZOOMER Magazine*. Created by Moses Znaimer and edited by Suzanne Boyd, *ZOOMER* has quickly become Canada's leading print medium for reaching boomers and seniors. (Disclosure: At the time of writing, I work for ZoomerMedia Limited, which owns the magazine as well as a portfolio of other media properties including TV, radio, and Internet, as well as consumer shows, all targeting this demographic.)

The media kit is designed to give potential advertisers information about the size and importance of this audience. You can see right off the bat that we're not talking about simply having more old people alive today. They're not the *same* old people as ever before. Their energy, activity, and spending power make them the dominant force in the marketplace.

ZoomerMedia has done the best job I've seen of rebranding the boomers and seniors, but the message of how potent this group is, and how differently they're behaving compared against previous norms and expectations, is certainly not unique to Canada.

My friend Brent Green, a Colorado-based marketing consultant and writer who focuses on baby boomers, has labeled them Generation Reinvention. I'll be referring to his book of the same name and some of his very important ideas more fully in the next chapter.

Another colleague of mine, Nancy Padberg, has created a media representation company called Navigate Boomer Media. The company sells advertising for a network of over 150 boomer-focused websites with a combined audience of more than two million people. Her website, <www.navigateboomermedia.com>, is filled with pictures of youthful-looking men and women, all of them using their computers to go online – for research, for connections, and especially for shopping. Take a moment to visit the site. Do you get the impression the audience is old? Passive? Out of touch? Afraid of technology?

In my first book, *The New Old*, I complained that a youth-obsessed Madison Avenue had not really woken up to the power of boomers and seniors in the marketplace. That was in late 2008. Today the situation is changing. We're not all the way there yet – there are still far too many ad agency types (particularly those who create the actual ads and commercials) who still have no clue about this audience. But on the client side, there is much more awareness now. There are books, blogs, conventions and trade shows, and associations – such as the International Mature Marketing Network – that are enabling professionals to exchange ideas and techniques. I have conducted a webinar for the last-named group, telling them about ZoomerMedia and our progress in Canada.

The growing interest in the 45-plus population as a market is very important to our story. Until very recently, the boomers and seniors exerted their clout without having it acknowledged. In fact, they were likely to be typecast as people who were aging in the same way as people had always aged – and they didn't like it one bit. You could write a whole book on reactions to the terms "senior" or "golden age" or "pensioner" – the notion that "aging" could only mean disengagement, helplessness, dependency.

But as the power of the 45-plus population is becoming more widely recognized, the recognition in and of itself is further reinforcing that power. (Conversely, as the weaknesses of the millennial generation are being more widely discussed in the marketplace of ideas, the discussion itself is serving to exacerbate those weaknesses.)

Mary Furlong is one of the pioneers in recognizing the importance of this market; she founded her marketing consultancy, geared specifically to the boomer and senior markets, all the way back in 2003. A look at her website <www.maryfurlong.com> reveals the topics she's dealing with:

- *The rise of gray tech*

- *Adults 74 and older who are online have quadrupled their social networking presence*

- *Aging in place 2.0*

- *The silver tsunami*

- *Launching start-ups in retirement*

"This bubble won't burst!" Furlong declares at the top of her home page. (And she's absolutely right – it's a mathematical certainty.) "You can tap into one of the world's largest and fastest-growing markets by reaching out to baby boomer and senior consumers."

The excitement derives not primarily from creating an image or rebranding "age," as interesting as that process is, but from the reality of the cash register – from concrete and substantial data that make the dominance of the 45-plus population crystal clear. So let's take a moment to nail down the actual facts and figures. I've chosen some of the key numbers from both the Canadian and American marketplaces.

Key Numbers: Canada

- There are 14.5 million Canadians over the age of 45, representing 57% of the adult population

- They account for almost 60% of all consumer spending, but in certain fast-growth categories, such as health and wellness, they dictate almost 80% of spending

- They represent 65% of all homeowners and 80% of all mortgage-free homeowners. They're the largest spenders on home improvement and renovation

- They completely dominate the financial marketplace, accounting for two-thirds of all those who personally hold stocks, mutual funds, and retirement savings plans. They represent about 70% of those who own investment real estate and 80% of those with total securities and savings of over $500,000

- They own 60% of all cars and buy more cars – new or used – than any other age group

- In the health, wellness, and beauty market, they account for 70% of all spending on over-the-counter remedies and almost 75% of all spending on prescription drugs

- They represent the largest market for all travel destinations – #1 for vacation travel within Canada, to the USA, to Europe, to Mexico and the Caribbean, and cruises to exotic destinations

- They attend concerts, theater, opera, museums, art galleries, and other public attractions more than any other age group. They read more books than any other age group

- In category after category – not just the obvious ones you would associate with aging – marketers have been forced to make boomers and seniors their *primary* targets in order to meet their sales objectives. (Here I must ask for the indulgence of professional marketers, who will note that I am omitting the more precise targeting that is necessary. There are numerous segments and sub-segments within the huge range of 45-plus; good marketers should, and do, drill down with much more exactitude than to categorize them simply as "boomers and seniors." But in the context of the Age Rage thesis, I am demonstrating the marketplace clout of the total 45-plus population.)

Key Numbers: USA

- There are 121 million Americans over the age of 45, representing 52% of the adult population

- They spend over $3.5 trillion a year, representing 58% of all consumer spending

- They control 70% of the total net worth in the USA – that's over $70 trillion of wealth in their hands

- They represent 60% of all health-care spending, and, as in Canada, over 70% of spending on prescription drugs

- They buy more than 50% of all new cars

- They account for more than 75% of all luxury vacations

- In 2010, annual spending by the 50-plus age group was 45% higher than it had been in 2000, while spending by those under 50 increased by just 6% over the entire decade

- And for those who think the boomers and seniors aren't all that engaged on the Internet, note that this group, in both countries, spent more money online last year than any other age group.

The Internet and the Generations

In fact, it's worth pausing to take a closer look at the Internet. Far beyond the value of e-commerce, the Internet is also the world's dominant marketplace for the exchange of ideas and the exercise of influence.

The millennials, of course, are completely engaged, and have been the first adapters of new technologies – social media, tablets, mobile apps. Boomers, and more so seniors, are seen as behind the curve, die-hard patrons of the dying off-line media models. Many argue that if the battle comes down to who is the most visible, or who can scream the loudest, the advantage in our new online world must go to the millennials.

Not so fast.

While it's true that the millennials are the first adapters, the boomers and seniors have not been all that far behind. It may be true that a higher percentage of millennials use the Internet and specific tools and applications. However, the boomer and senior percentages are high enough that, when multiplied by the much higher absolute numbers represented by the 45-plus population, the *size* of the 45-plus online population dwarfs that of the millennials.

The Canadian numbers illustrate the point very clearly. Based on a variety of government and industry sources, the consensus of Internet usage in 2011, by age groups, is approximately as follows.

Internet Usage in 2011 by Age Groups			
18-24 90%	25-34 85%	35-44 80%	45+ 70%

Comparing the millennials with the combo of boomers and seniors, it looks like a meaningful spread – 20 percentage points. But not when you factor in the absolute size of each age group.

Internet Usage in 2011 by Age Groups: Absolute Numbers				
	18-24	25-34	35-44	45-plus
Number of people in the age group (in millions)	3.2	4.5	4.8	14.5
% of Internet usage	90	85	80	70
Number of Internet users (in millions)	2.9	3.8	3.8	10.2

Even if every single one of those aged 18 to 24 years old were online, as an age group they would contribute – *could* contribute – only three million Internet users to the total Canadian Internet population. The 45-plus age group, with only a 70% online rate, contributes over 10 million Internet users ... *more than three times the size of the youngest group.*

The US rate of Internet usage, particularly among the 65-plus segment of the 45-plus population, is lower than the Canadian participation rate, but once again the sheer numerical advantage of the 45-plus segment produces a larger online population – well over 10 million – than the younger age groups.

Now of course "Internet usage" covers a very wide range. Some people could be online almost constantly; others could be online only occasionally. In percentage terms, it seems clear that the millennials use the Internet for more purposes, and with greater frequency, than any other age group. But it's equally clear that the 45-plus population not only spends more money online, but also uses the Internet as a potent tool for research leading to behavior. They are the heaviest online seekers of information on health, travel, finances, and lifestyle. The convenience of the Internet, and the ability to access information and compare information, plays right into the determination of the 45-plus population to keep control of their lives and to actively manage the process of aging to gain a higher quality of life for as long as possible. This is extending now to social media: Those 45-plus are the fastest-growing group on Facebook, and they are rapidly learning how to use the Internet for social and political influence.

My point is that if the millennials have any advantage as early adopters of new technology, they will not be able to leverage it in any meaningful way. They are already heavily outnumbered in the online world; the nooks and crannies they may still occupy for a brief time before the boomers and seniors get there will not be sufficient to give them a competitive advantage in the battle ahead.

To sum up, then, it is obvious that the boomers and seniors outgun any other age group. They have the numbers. They have the spending power. What's more, their attitudes directly contradict all previous patterns of how older people behave and are expected to behave.

These attitudes are a critical component of our story – so critical that they demand a chapter of their own.

Boomers and Seniors: Attitudes

The Old Old

In 1927, the Liberal government of William Lyon Mackenzie King created Canada's first Old Age Pension.

The pension didn't kick in for people until they reached age 70, meaning the average recipient would start receiving funds when they had only about five more years of life expectancy. The benefits were remarkably stingy – only $20 a month (in today's dollars, an annual payout of less than $4,000). And to collect even that measly amount, you had to go through a means test. You were ineligible if your total annual income, *including the pension*, exceeded set limits.

And what were those set limits? A single pensioner could not go above $365. A married pensioner whose spouse was not receiving a pension was limited to $490. A two-pension couple could not exceed $730. And these are *annual* incomes, remember.

From today's perspective, we would call this mean, tight-fisted, penny-pinching, grudging, Dickensian – we wouldn't exactly be struggling for adjectives. But the recipients of the day, by all accounts, were grateful. The program was wildly popular. Mackenzie King touted it to great advantage politically. Some members of the Conservative opposition ruefully complained that the government was throwing buckets of money at old men to buy their votes.

I'm not making a point here about the pensions themselves. No matter how niggardly the benefits, or how demeaning the collection process, it was certainly a vital first step that would have a huge long-term impact, especially as the payouts were improved. What counts for our purposes is the reaction of the pensioners themselves, pocketing their few pennies with a humble smile, thankful to receive a pittance for the handful of years they had left.

The "old old," if you will. Powerless. Dependent on the kindness of strangers. Tipping their caps and shuffling offstage with a minimum of fuss.

The New Old

The situation couldn't be more different today. The oldest baby boomer is eligible for a Canada pension in 2011. The coming flood will not be passive and grateful. They'll be fighting for even more, and provoking their parents, the 65-plus seniors, to be just as feisty. They will be transferring to the public policy arena the same clout they exert in the commercial marketplace. It's already happening. As I am proofreading these pages, Canada's boomers and seniors are aroused by the Harper government's declaration that the Canadian pension system will have to be adjusted. I'll go into further detail about this in the chapter on political clout.

Some of this more aggressive posture, as we've already noted, may be attributed to increased longevity. People with decades left to live don't act the same as those with only a few years to go.

But longevity doesn't explain everything. For the rest of the picture, we have to understand the baby boomers, the unique generation that is driving this profound revolution in the very nature of aging.

Thanks to the boomers, there are new terms and definitions, new expectations, new patterns of behavior that have never been seen before. A century from now, when the human life span may have been pushed toward 150 or even beyond, radically different attitudes, systems, and institutions will reflect the new reality. The baby boomers are the advance guard of all the changes that are coming. They're creating the new paths, sometimes taking a machete to the undergrowth, sometimes bypassing obstacles to find never-explored trails. Their influence spills upward, too; that is, they are exerting a big impact on the older age cohorts – 70-plus, 80-plus, 90-plus.

Boomers Behaving Badly

Few, if any, generations have been as closely studied or as widely written about as the baby boomers, perhaps because at every age they have passed through, they represented the most important segment of the consumer marketplace at that time.

A solid consensus exists, too. Nobody likes the boomers.

Their attitudes and conduct are widely seen in a negative light, even by boomers themselves.

Let me kick off with excerpts from Paul Begala's famous diatribe, which I also quoted in *The New Old*. An advisor to Bill Clinton and still a prominent political consultant and commentator, Begala was born in 1961, so he's actually a late baby boomer himself. No matter. He unloads big:

> *I hate the Baby Boomers. They're the most self-centered, self-seeking, self-interested, self-absorbed, self-indulgent, self-aggrandizing generation in American history. As they enter late middle age, the Boomers still can't grow up ...*

And on and on, even including a diatribe about boomer music:

> *And don't give me this crap about Boomer music ...*
> *The generation that came before the Boomers gave them*

Dylan. The Boomers gave us KC and the Sunshine Band. Thanks a lot.

It's a wonderful rant, filled with a disdain that is almost delicious in its exuberance.

Inspired by Begala, I went on to Google and typed in "Baby boomers are selfish." I got back over 750,000 results and didn't have to go too deeply into the pile to find vivid examples of how just how unloved the boomers are.

Here is Francis Beckett in *The Guardian*, in the summer of 2010. The headline is "Baby Boomers: Powerful and Selfish," and the subtitle reads, "We've had the best of times. Now we're using our voting muscle to ensure our children inherit a far harsher world." Beckett goes on to say:

> *We had the freedom that comes from not having to fear starvation if your employer fires you: there were other jobs to go to, and a welfare state to fall back on. These things made possible the freedom of the 60s.*
>
> *And what did we do with this wonderful inheritance? We trashed it.*
>
> *We created a far harsher world for our children to grow up in. It was as though we decided that the freedom and lack of worry which we had inherited was too good for our children, and we pulled up the ladder we had climbed.*

Here's Peter Oborne, writing in the *Daily Mail*, again in 2010. Under the headline "So Long, Losers! How the Baby Boomers Took the Money and Ran," he reviews a book called *The Pinch*, by British politician David Willetts, who argues that the baby boomers have destroyed the implied contract between generations. Oborne agrees, in unmistakable terms.

> *We Baby Boomers have been the most selfish generation that history has ever known. We could have used our*

> *gigantic piece of demographic good fortune to build for the future. Instead, we have spent every last penny of our windfall gain. Indeed, we have done even worse than that. We have incurred gigantic debts that will have to be paid off by future generations – who will already be reeling under the necessity of paying for the largest number of pensioners in history.*

Both of these examples come from Britain, and it's striking that both writers (like Paul Begala) are themselves baby boomers.

Now, by way of balance, here are a few comments from younger generations, in North America.

Writer and blogger Sherri Souzen, who says she is speaking from the perspective of a Generation X member (child of the boomers), writes:

> *The Baby Boomers enjoyed the luxury of choosing a self-actualizing career, and in fact they made it de rigueur. As parents and teachers, they taught us, Generation X, that we, too, could choose any career we wanted ... In fact, we could even have kids when we wanted, there's no hurry ... But most of all, we could succeed if only we tried, as they did.*
>
> *We could have it all.*
>
> *What they didn't tell us was that, yes, we could have it all ... as soon as they were done with it.*

Here's a rant posted on Free Republic all the way back in 2003:

> *The Baby Boomers are arguably the most short-sighted and self-interested generation that America has ever seen but they are in the majority so there is no-one to stop them. I'm even certain that they will come up with some grand rationalization about why I should be thrilled to pay the bill for them one more time.*

And here's something from an entire blog devoted to hating baby boomers. In fact, that's the URL, <www.ihateboomers.net>.

> *As an American born during the perceived quality of life decline in the USA, I am appalled at the rhetoric, language and condescending demeanor used by the Baby Boomers. The most wasteful generation in the history of the world, let alone the USA, has forever altered our environment, culture, politics and overall way of life in a permanent way.*

I've cherry-picked, of course, but trust me when I say I could have you wallowing in this invective for hundreds of pages.

Self-absorption to the point of narcissism. Self-aggrandizement. Greed. Irresponsibility. Leaving a mess for others to clean up. Accusations hurled not only across the generations, but also by members of the generation itself.

Adaptive Boomers

Are the boomers really that bad?

In one sense, I suppose I should argue that they are, because that would certainly reinforce the thesis of Age Rage. The selfish baby boomers refuse to leave the stage not only for reasons of culture or attitude ("We're still hot, we'll always be hot"), but also for the grubbier reason of money ("We want, we want, we want"). They hog the available resources. They lay a claim on future resources. They pitilessly elbow their own children and grandchildren out of the way.

Talk about a relentless army. I could simply leave it at that and say, "You see? You see?"

But it would be wrong to leave it at this one-dimensional level.

For one thing, the picture is not as black and white as the avalanche of lurid quotes would lead us to believe. If the baby boomers are self-absorbed, they are also the generation that pushed for civil rights, equality for women, concern for the environment. They stopped the war in Vietnam. They opened up academia and the workplace to minorities on a scale like never before.

(And, with all due respect to Paul Begala, I would put Freddy Mercury, Bruce Springsteen, Elton John, Billy Joel, Linda Ronstadt, John Fogerty, Michael Jackson, Madonna, David Bowie, Andrew Lloyd Webber, and Stevie Wonder on any music list and not feel embarrassed. Not to mention ABBA, Emmylou Harris, Sting, Eric Clapton, and Pete Townshend.)

Second, and more importantly, since the boomers are still in action, their attitudes and behaviors are still fluid. They are responding (both willingly and of necessity) to drastically new conditions they could not have foreseen back in the heady days of "make love, not war." They are still writing the book on their generation.

This second point is very critical in the context of Age Rage.

Yes, the boomers and their parents collectively make up the largest and wealthiest age group in society. Yes, they are trying to flex that muscle to keep the pension and health-care benefits they need and feel entitled to. And yes, that is causing an apparent war with the younger generations.

But – and it's a big "but" – even if they grabbed more than their fair share of the public purse, that still wouldn't throw off enough money to satisfy their requirements. As we will see in more detail in the coming chapter, the boomers are seriously underfunded and would be even if the economy weren't in trouble. They're being forced to adjust, to adapt. They're staying in the workforce, or launching second (or third) careers. Being boomers, of course, they can characterize this as just another nifty aspect of boomerhood. They can spin it as a positive innovation rather than an act of desperate necessity. Clinging to a job becomes "reinventing retirement."

But there's more than boomer ego at play here. The boomers really do have strong adaptive skills, an astonishing ability to change direction, to get out ahead of events and set new trends. They've been doing it all their lives. My colleague Brent Green, a Colorado-based marketing consultant with an incisive understanding of where the boomer market is going, describes them as Generation Reinvention. They have always been the generation who reinvented – not only themselves, but also the society around them.

His book by the same name describes how boomers are changing "business, marketing, aging and the future." That's quite an agenda, but he makes the case conclusively. "Whichever life stage boomers have occupied," he says, "collectively they've transformed business and mainstream values." As he goes on to demonstrate:

- *When they were children, the country became obsessively child-centric, as exemplified by TV hit shows such as* Leave It to Beaver *and* Father Knows Best *and* The Brady Bunch. *Hula Hoops, Slinkys, and GI Joe became colossal fads.*

- *When they were teenagers, they developed a taste for sugar, salt, and saturated fat. To satisfy teen cravings and unrelenting hunger pangs, McDonald's grew from a single California store to an international French-frying juggernaut.*

- *When they entered college, they pursued agendas of government accountability, racial equality, multiculturalism, feminism, egalitarian values, and environmental awareness. The Volkswagen Beetle became a mega-brand, equally iconoclastic and inclusive.*

- *When they were Yuppies during the high-flying 1980s and 1990s, Boomers charted new vistas for consumer materialism, latching onto BMWs and high-growth mutual funds. Children again took center stage as Boomer parents trekked to daycare with kids protectively shrouded in SUVs sporting "Baby on Board" placards.*

And so it goes for the future. Boomers will redefine the autumnal and winter life stages, stretching the limits of what it means to be 50, 60, 70, 80, 90, and, for an expected two million of them in the United States, 100. New mega-brands will be born.

So it isn't just a matter of boomers suddenly making a virtue out of necessity and developing "reinvention" as a way to make hip a behavior that is really founded on good old-fashioned dollars and cents. Yes, the need for those dollars and cents provides an element of urgency to new attitudes and behaviors – and it's not a small element, either. But throughout their lives the boomers have repeatedly changed gears – for instance, going from Woodstock to Wall Street in less than a decade – in order to satisfy what Green calls "their innermost impulses for reinvention and control of destiny." Boomers have always been comfortable changing costumes. Boomers have always been quick to identify trends at their most embryonic stage and then to own those trends and ride them to their own benefit.

Millennials, by contrast, have no such prior experience or tradition. In the struggle that is already unfolding, they will find it difficult to be as adaptive as the boomers.

The Boomers' Ringside Seat

One last factor must be noted. The boomers, as a generation, not only are the leaders in developing new attitudes and responses to aging, but they also are the middlemen for a host of converging influences brought on by increased longevity:

- The sandwich effect: Boomers are simultaneously looking after the care of their still-living parents and providing, as we will see, care to their children (and often, grandchildren)
- Health-care reform: Boomers are conscious not only of their own growing health-care needs, but also, through

caring for their parents, of the deficiencies of the health-care system. This has caused them to morph from "patient" to "consumer" and driven them, with a lot of help from the Internet, to research health-care alternatives and to be more proactive in trying to control health-care outcomes for themselves and their parents

- Independent living: Market research suggests that boomers and their parents fear going into a nursing home *more than they fear death*. The nursing home industry is responding with a variety of new formats and services, while technology is also producing new products that promote "aging in place" (for example, ultra-sophisticated sensors that allow for remote monitoring of the frail elderly). Boomers are the major target market for these products and services, giving them another important window into what's coming and reinforcing a thought process that focuses on new ideas and solutions

These are just three examples, but they're enough to make the point: Even without already being attitudinally predisposed to change or "reinvention," the boomers by circumstance have a ringside seat to new ideas, products, and services that are the direct result of longer life spans. They are being forced to confront situations that have never existed before – multigenerational responsibilities, changing roles in health care, the use of technology to extend life (and, equally important, quality of life), and new formats in housing and living arrangements. This stimulates their already strong interest, and skill, in changing, in getting out ahead of new developments, and above all (and here we go back to the boomer ego) in being in control.

I have spent some time on the attitude piece because I think it's just as important as numbers or purchasing power – and in the context of a war, maybe even more important. It means the boomers, carrying the seniors with them, field an army not only with firepower but also with morale – an army that can read the landscape, spot the opportunities, adjust to changing circumstances.

But what are the goals of this army? What are they after? And why does this necessarily mean a war with the millennials?

Boomers and Seniors: Objectives

*O*NE evening in the winter of 2006, I took part in a very interesting focus group. We were talking to people between the ages of 60 and 75 – old enough not to think of themselves as "young" any more, but not so old that they couldn't be making plans for the future (and therefore, by discussing those plans, revealing their hopes, fears, and other attitudes).

We ran four groups that night, involving a total of about 60 people. We started off each group with the question, "Looking ahead, what is your biggest fear?"

Every single one of the respondents provided exactly the same answer.

Care to take a guess what the answer was? Write your guess in the space below (no peeking).

Looking ahead, what is your biggest fear?
All respondents said:

....

What did you guess? Death? Disease? Helplessness?

Okay, here's the actual answer:

> **Looking ahead, what is your biggest fear?**
> **All respondents said:**
> *Outliving my money...*

Note the date – 2006. *Before* the economic crash and stock market meltdown, yet the fear was already there.

This anecdote demonstrates that the economic anxieties of the boomer/senior combo are based on deep fundamentals and not just the unexpected calamity of October 2008.

And it is these economic anxieties that are making the 45-plus age group behave as an army, are bringing that army onto the field, and are creating logical "enemies," contesting some of the same terrain.

As with all of the issues we are looking at, longevity alone provides some of the explanation: "The good news is, you're going to live longer. The bad news is, you're going to live longer."

Living longer requires more money, obviously, and it puts a huge amount of pressure on you to have accumulated enough money to keep you going (in a reasonable state of health and well-being) once you've retired.

There's nothing controversial about this notion; it is self-evident.

Let's say you retire at the traditional age of 65 and have to live off your accumulated savings and pensions. In the 1950s, based on average North American life expectancies, you would have had to sustain yourself for a little more than a decade. Today, it's about 16 to 18 years, but with advances in medicine it's pushing toward 20 years and maybe longer. (Remember, the fastest-growing age group is that of the centenarians.)

And don't forget, the *psychology* of a longer life expectancy is stronger than the actual statistics. If you're 65 today, you have a plausible shot at 90. If you've retired (the traditional or expected behavior), you have 25 more years of *not* earning an employment income and relying on accumulated wealth and the cash flow of ongoing pensions. The fact that you may not make it, *statistically*, that you may die earlier and be one of those who are bringing the average in at the mid-80s, doesn't really affect your thought process very much as you survey the world at age 65. You see more and more people who *are* making it, into their late 80s, their 90s, and beyond.

So if you look at your employment as stopping at 65, and contemplate whether or not you're in the financial shape to sustain another quarter century of living, it's easy to be apprehensive ... even if you're in good shape. You're probably thinking, "Do I really have enough for 30 more years?"

Hint: No.

Even without the 2008 disaster, the baby boomers were already seriously underfunded in terms of their ability to retire with sufficient security.

And as for the seniors – the 65-plus segment – the 2008 wipeout devastated their retirement funds, either through losses in their investment portfolios, the destruction of the value of their home (home equity being the retirement nest egg most of them had been counting on), or loss of or cutbacks to expected pension benefits. Or a combination of all three.

The net net? The 45-plus population is seriously short of the cash they need to sustain an acceptable, let alone lavish, lifestyle going forward. The good news of their added longevity only intensifies the bad news of their need for more cash.

Just how bad is the shortfall?

In Canada, only 20% of baby boomers have savings of $250,000 or more, according to research by Michael Adams, founder of Environics and author of *Stayin' Alive: How Canadian Baby Boomers Will Work, Play, and Find Meaning in the Second Half of Their Adult Lives*. About a third have savings of less than $100,000. What's more, almost a quarter of the older boomers (born between 1946 and 1955) will have debts of over $50,000 when they stop working.

Almost a third of Canadians over the age of 65 have no retirement savings or private pension benefits and will be entirely dependent on the public pension plan and income supplement, plus whatever they can earn or scrounge.

It's even worse in the USA. Younger baby boomers (below the age of 55) have average retirement savings (as of 2011) of only $30,000. Half of the boomers over the age of 55 have less than $50,000 in retirement savings; in fact, almost 40% of them have less than $25,000 and 20% have less than $5,000. It's been estimated that close to 70% of baby boomers will have to keep working (at least part-time) past the age of 65 *just to cover basic expenses.*

If all this wasn't bad enough, there are massive problems with federal and state pension plans. The federal Social Security system now pays out more than it takes in, and, according to the most recent estimates, it could run out of money (unless benefits are cut) as early as 2036. The 50 states combined have *unfunded* pension liabilities, for their retired employees, totaling more than $1 trillion – if nothing else, this is a recipe for fierce fighting over who will get what.

Retirees will need every dime, too, because there's much less slack, or margin for error, in household budgets than there used to be. This is vividly illustrated in data from Statistics Canada comparing the spending patterns of Canadians over the age of 55 in 1982 and 2003. If we view "savings" as the discretionary amount left over after the essentials have been covered, it's instantly clear that the room to maneuver has been shrinking steadily. Add to that the factor of increased longevity (one more time), the need to keep the package together for years, maybe decades, more than ever before, and it isn't difficult to understand the intensity of 45-plus anxiety ... and motivation.

Spending Patterns by Age Groups: Amounts Saved Per Dollar						
	Ages 55-64		Ages 65-74		Ages 75+	
	1982	2003	1982	2003	1982	2003
Total disbursed	100	100	100	100	100	100
Personal consumption	59	67	69	74	62	71
Income tax	17	22	10	16	9	11
Security	4	5	3	3	0	1
Gifts, contributions	4	3	5	3	7	6
Savings	16	3	13	4	22	10

As you can see, the youngest group, ages 55 to 64, had 16 cents out of every dollar left over for savings in 1982 and only 3 cents in 2003. That's a drop of 81%. Those in the 65 to 74 age group could pocket 13 cents out of every dollar in 1982 and only 4 cents in 2003, a drop of 69%. The oldest group, 75-plus, which you might intuitively expect to be the best at penny-pinching, saved almost a quarter on every dollar in 1982 and only a dime in 2003. They beat the other groups – if you can call it a win – by holding their decline to "only" 54%.

The cash squeeze creates two instant and unambiguous objectives for the 45-plus population:

- Bring in more cash

- Fight to keep every penny of whatever pension or other financial benefits you may already be getting

Light these two fires under the backside of a generation of people who have been demanding and hyper-aggressive all their lives, who are used to having things their own way, who are experienced at driving change in society, and the resulting behaviors should come as absolutely no surprise.

And if this weren't enough, we can light a third fire – health care.

Canada and the USA have very different health-care systems, yet both share the same underlying problem: They are financially unsustainable. The pressures to reform will be decisive – it's a simple matter of arithmetic – and the nature of the reforms will bring the boomers and their parents into the field to protect their existing entitlements and future interests.

It's very important to note that the Age Rage thesis does *not* depend on the specifics of what future health-care reforms will be. Canada may or may not end up keeping its single-payer system, or may be forced to move to a mixed public-private model. The USA may or may not retain its private-public model, or may move to more government funding, particularly for those who cannot obtain private insurance.

A vast literature, in both countries, argues for different models and different reforms, coming at the problem from left, right, and centrist points of view. It is not our job, in this book, to wade into the details of those arguments. It's enough, for our purposes, to demonstrate that change is coming and that many possible versions of that change will be seen as threatening to the boomers and seniors. This threat is already mobilizing them, and the intensity is only going to increase.

What's more, health care is one topic in which the interests of the boomers and seniors have implications that could threaten the interests of the millennials, particularly in Canada. The reason is simple: Health care is the number-one spending item for every province in Canada, and the number-two item is education. The pressure to maintain or increase government funding of health care automatically creates a pressure not to maintain or increase spending on education. True, the countervailing pressures may be reconciled by cutting spending in other areas, apart from health care or education, but even if compromises can be found, the head-to-head debate is going to happen, and it will exacerbate intergenerational conflict.

Worse yet, in some of the more pessimistic scenarios, future health-care spending is indeed maintained, thanks to the political clout of the boomers and seniors, but only through higher tax rates to be suffered by the millennials (and those who are today even younger). To the degree that much of health-care spending is focused on end-of-life costs, the anger and resentment of the younger generations will only increase: They will be infuriated at having to pay higher taxes than the boomers themselves had to pay. And at having to do so to fund a health-care system that devotes an increasingly larger percentage of its costs toward helping boomers (today's seniors by then having already passed from the scene) add only a handful of years to their already-long life spans.

These thoughts and resentments are already being voiced, as we will see. Again, for our purposes it doesn't matter whether the actual costs and burdens will turn out as envisaged – many argue persuasively that the boomers will not be a burden, and that new models of prevention and wellness will emerge, reducing end-of-life costs – but only that the arguments and conflicts are in play today and are providing fuel to the competing armies.

The policy alternatives now under debate may be wide ranging, but there is really no argument that the current health-care models in both Canada and the USA are financially unsupportable. Let's look at some of the details in both countries.

Canadian Health-care Realities

Canada's public health-care system is administered by the provinces, with additional funding support from the federal government. The system covers only physician and basic hospital services, for which private alternatives are normally not allowed. Other health-care services, such as dentistry and prescription drugs, lie outside the public system, although the provinces do subsidize certain prescription drugs under various provincial drug benefit plans that target the needs of seniors.

Between 1975 and 2009, total Canadian spending on health care (in 1997 dollars) more than tripled, from $40 billion to just under $140 billion. On a per capita basis, the jump was from about $1,700 to $4,000. In current dollars, total spending is in the $200 billion range, or about $5,400 per person.

Government spending covers about 70% of this total, and about 90% of that spending comes from the provinces.

But the federal top-up is decisive. Between 1997 and 2007, the feds provided just under $120 billion a year to the provinces. Without this money, the provinces would have been in even worse shape.

As it is, including federal funding, health-care spending is already eating up over 40% of provincial budgets today, and costs are rising faster than revenues. If the provinces paid for health care through their "own source" revenues, without the federal top-up, their spending on health care would actually be above 50%.

There is no way the provinces can continue on this trajectory.

Provinces are dealing with the crunch by rationing services – e.g., creating wait times that increasingly come under public scrutiny and complaint – and by juggling the number of prescription drugs they will cover under their provincial drug benefit plans, which provide subsidies to seniors. Currently provincial plans cover less than 25% of all drugs approved by Health Canada. There are rational and non-controversial reasons to exclude many individual drugs – particularly drugs that deal with chronic conditions (e.g., high blood pressure) where there are multiple options and generic substitutions and where it is certainly not necessary to cover every single brand name prescription drug that is on the market. But as new drug therapies continue to be developed, in categories such as cancer and Alzheimer's disease, we can expect even more intense pressure on provincial health-care budgets. This in turn will increase the focus on health-care policy and who gets what.

The federal government has just retooled the formula under which it subsidizes provincial health-care spending. Where observers had expected a long and complex renegotiation of the existing formula (the Canada Health Accord, scheduled to expire in 2014), the feds pre-empted the process by announcing they would continue to increase health transfer payments to the provinces by 6 percent annually for the next six years, but at that point would start linking transfer dollars to the rate of economic growth and inflation, although increases would never fall below 3 percent. As well, there would be less federal control over how the funds were spent, leaving it up to each province to innovate.

This will gradually transform health-care delivery into a number of models that may differ by province – putting even more of a premium on the organization of political clout that will be necessary to influence ten provinces and not just the feds. Guess which army has that level of organization and clout?

American Health-care Realities

Contrary to popular belief (especially in Canada), the USA does not have an all-private health-care system. The federal government funds Medicare, which provides health care for people 65 years and older and for certain people with disabilities under the age of 65. There are also other federal programs covering the very poor and children in certain circumstances, including Medicaid and various health and hospital programs for military veterans.

For our purposes, the most important program to look at is Medicare. As of 2010, this program covered a total of 48 million Americans, of which 40 million were aged 65 or over.

Medicare has four parts. Part A covers hospital treatment, Part B covers medical treatment, and Part D covers prescription drugs. There is a Part C, also known as Medicare Advantage, which is a mechanism for beneficiaries to receive their Medicare benefits through private insurance health plans. For all parts of Medicare, there is a bewildering array of rules, exceptions, co-payments, and other terms and conditions that need not bog us down here.

Medicare is paid for through two trust funds held by the United States Treasury. The funds may be used only for Medicare payments. The first trust fund, the Hospital Insurance Trust, pays for Medicare Part A and is funded through payroll taxes and a few other sources such as income taxes paid on Social Security benefits, interest earned from the trust funds themselves, and certain premiums paid by people who are not eligible for premium-free Part A benefits. The second trust fund, the Supplementary Insurance Medical Trust Fund, pays out the benefits under Part B and Part D and is funded through premiums collected from people enrolled in Part B and Part D and by additional funds authorized by Congress.

The two funds disbursed $522.8 billion in 2010, which was $36.8 billion *more than they took in.* So the program is already under water. The trustees issued a very bleak outlook in their report for 2011, which is also a comment on the Social Security program:

The financial conditions of the Social Security and Medicare programs remain challenging. Projected long-run program costs for both Medicare and Social Security are not sustainable under currently scheduled financing, and will require legislative modifications if disruptive consequences for beneficiaries and taxpayers are to be avoided.

The long-run financial challenges facing Social Security and Medicare should be addressed soon. If action is taken sooner rather than later, more options and more time will be available to phase in changes so that those affected have adequate time to prepare. Earlier action will also afford elected officials with a greater opportunity to minimize adverse impacts on vulnerable populations, including lower-income workers and those who are already substantially dependent on program benefits.

Both Social Security and Medicare, the two largest federal programs, face substantial cost growth in the upcoming decades due to factors that include population aging as well as the growth in expenditures per beneficiary. Through the mid-2030s, due to the large baby-boom generation entering retirement and lower-birth-rate generations entering employment, population aging is the largest single factor contributing to cost growth in the two programs. Thereafter, the continued rapid growth in health care cost per beneficiary becomes the larger factor.

How bad is it?

The trustees predict that, absent changes in the programs, the Medicare trust funds will run out of money in 2024. (Just a year earlier, in their report for 2010, they were predicting that the program could hang on until 2029 – so you can see how quickly and dramatically the situation is eroding.) Social Security is expected to run out in 2036.

Bear in mind, too, that the demography is inexorable. As of 2010, about 40 million Americans aged 65-plus are covered under Medicare. By 2031, when the last of the baby boomers hit 65, a total of *80 million* will be covered (if Medicare, in its present form, is still there). The required payroll taxes will take a big hit over that period: In 2010, there were 3.5 workers for every recipient of Medicare benefits; in 2031, the ratio will drop to 2.3:1.

The Drama Unfolds

So we have all the ingredients for high drama – high stakes, dwindling resources, and a deadline for action.

The issue is already galvanizing boomers and seniors, and we'll explore their opening moves in the next section of this book. Bear in mind that the issue impacts boomers not only because of their fears concerning what they may or may not collect in the future but also because of their immediate concerns concerning what they may have to cough up if their parents' benefits are in any way eroded. As if they don't have enough financial pressures due to their own lack of retirement funding, they now have to worry about what will happen to their still-living parents in the short and medium term.

And this goes beyond dollars and cents. There are important quality-of-life issues attached to possible cutbacks in healthcare coverage, and since much of the burden of caregiving falls on the baby boomers, this draws them into the future of healthcare debate in an urgent way that transcends their concerns for their own immediate state of health.

As we can see, then, the boomers and seniors have a very concrete and anxiety-producing agenda. They can see that most or all of their assumptions about retirement and retirement funding are not coming to pass. They can see that some of the key programs and institutions that they were counting on to provide relief may not be sustainable going forward. They can even begin to see the clash of generations – most notably in Europe, where collectors of pensions and other social benefits are pitted against unemployed youth.

The choice – sit back and hope for the best, or get involved and take control of how the dollars are going to be allocated – isn't a difficult one, particularly for the boomers. They've never been shy about asserting their claims and protecting their interests. And they've always had thick skins when it came to the pejorative labels attached to them by jealous or disgruntled members of other generations.

When decisions are made about how the pie is going to be sliced, the boomers will make sure they're the ones holding the knife.

Which doesn't bode well for the other contenders, the millennials.

Millennials: The Kids Are Not All Right

*G*****IVEN*** their collective size, skills, and energy – and the urgency of their cause – the boomers and seniors would be a formidable enough opponent against even the toughest and most organized adversary. Against millennials, it's no contest.

I'm not exactly adventuring into risky territory by criticizing the millennials. They don't – let's be honest – get a great press.

Here, for example, is Judith Warner of the *New York Times*, in a 2010 article under the heading "The Why-Worry Generation."

> *For the past few years, it's been open season on Generation Y – also known as the millennials, echo boomers or, less flatteringly, Generation Me. One described by trend-watchers Neil Howe and William Strauss as "the next great generation" – optimistic, idealistic and destined to do good – millennials, born between 1982 and 2002, have been depicted more recently by employers, professors and earnestly concerned mental-health experts as entitled whiners who have been spoiled by parents who overstoked their self-esteem, teachers who granted undeserved A's and sports coaches who bestowed trophies on any player who showed up.*

And here is Patricia Sellers, writing on the *Fortune* magazine website, also in 2010, under the headline, "Who Cares About a Career? Not Gen Y."

> *Any Baby Boomer who has worked alongside millennials – Gen Yers born after 1978 – knows how differently they view work and career. While we Baby Boomers typically place high value on pay, benefits, stability and prestige, Gen Y cares most about fun, innovation, social responsibility and time off.*

Here's what Canadian professors Ken Coates and Bill Morrison say in their 2011 book *Campus Confidential: 100 Startling Things You Don't Know About Canadian Universities*:

> *A decade ago, faculty members at a Maritime university started complaining over coffee about their students' behavior in the class: inconsistent attendance, lack of respect for professors, poor classroom behavior, litigiousness, and a reluctance to complete assignments. At a meeting with high school counselors, they asked the obvious question: "What is going on with the current group of students?" The reply was unexpected: "If you think this is bad, wait until you see the Grade 9's that are coming."*

Together, Coates and Morrison bring over 90 years' experience to this topic as professors, deans, and senior administrators at universities across Canada and in the USA. They've seen previous generations of students; they've seen the normal patterns of freshmen-level unpreparedness and gradual maturing. So if they believe today is different, there's good reason for alarm. They write:

> *Every generation claims that the next one has been coddled and spoiled, but it really may be true this time. There are dozens of explanations for the remarkable*

freedom, high expectations, and unreasonable demands of today's youth. There's the guilt and the money of two-income families, societal permissiveness, child-centered educational and parental styles, overwhelming materialism, video games, sexualized media, and on and on.

The changes in the student psyche are not all bad, of course. These "spoiled" students are more assertive, very confident, able and willing to express their opinions, not intimidated by adults and professors, and very sure of themselves.

But they also have a deep sense of entitlement. They expect material well-being and an easy passage through school, university and work. They expect a great deal from their professors and university staff and can be quite nasty if those expectations are not met. Their evaluations of their profs can be devastating.

They often expect deadlines to be altered, want their explanations accepted without confirmation, and try to insist that course requirements fit their availability to do work. Not all students fit this description, but the general student population has changed.

They sum it all up in one scathing sentence: "Eighteen is the new fifteen."

Their book should be required reading for parents and for anyone concerned with the future of our university system.

Ken Coates answered some of my questions specifically for this book. I'll present his observations later in this chapter.

Criticism of the millennials doesn't come only from tut-tutting elders. Here is 25-year-old David N. Bass, for example, writing for *American Spectator* under the inflammatory title, "Diapers for 26-Year-Olds." He acknowledges that macro-economic forces may be responsible for a lot of the grief the millennials are suffering, but then says:

Young people ... are also lagging because of self-inflicted wounds. Massive student-loan debt, high consumer credit card balances, frequent changing of jobs because of boredom, poor work ethic, entitlement attitudes, heightened standard-of-living expectations, preoccupation with self-esteem, and delay of marriage and parenthood.

Of course the millennials do have their supporters. In 2006, Anya Kamenetz (then only four years out of Yale) wrote *Generation Debt: Why Now Is a Terrible Time to Be Young*. While the book lays out a very bleak future for the millennials (and trends since then have certainly not proved her wrong), Kamenetz provides a well-researched and brilliantly argued defense of her generation, along with no-nonsense advice on how they can overcome their obstacles. (Advice that, alas, does not appear to have been taken.) This author also agreed to answer questions from me, and they are presented later in the chapter.

Kamenetz acknowledges in her book that millennials get a bad rap from their elders and pushes back vigorously:

> *It really makes me angry to see the Boomers in charge of the media and other powerful institutions attributing the problems young people are going through to nothing more serious than a lack of initiative. Collectively, the mass media have stamped an image of eighteen-to-thirty-four-year-olds as slackers, overgrown children, and procrastinators, as though we're intentionally dragging our heels to avoid reaching adulthood ...*
>
> *This attitude is especially insufferable because it's arguably our elders who are taking far more than their fair share ... Instead of saving enough for their own retirement, let alone for our future, the Boomers are going into deeper debt than any generation before them. Because of their projected retirement expenses, the entire nation is going bankrupt, with a total accumulate funding*

gap in the federal budget that's greater than our national net worth. Who's going to be around when that bill comes due? Young people.

She may be absolutely correct – but for our purposes, it really doesn't matter where the blame lies. We could even concede, if we wanted to push it to the extreme, that none of the fault lies with the millennials themselves; that they're entirely the victims of influences and circumstances not of their own making – the sins of their parents and grandparents, compounded by exquisitely bad timing concerning when to come into the world.

But shifting the blame doesn't change the reality of how badly the millennial army stacks up against the boomers and seniors. Looking at the causes, however, does help us to better understand that reality. Just as a number of factors coalesced at the same moment to make the boomers and seniors more powerful (and more aggressive), so a number of factors have combined to make the millennials so weak.

We've already looked at some of those factors – those that have to do with larger social and economic forces, and with the boomers and seniors themselves. We've noted that the millennials have the bad luck to be hitting young adulthood at the same moment a worldwide economic crisis is threatening the entire premise of the Western social democratic model (even its relatively minimalist version in the USA). There is an acute shortage of jobs. The financial resources (state and private) that used to be able to satisfy everybody are melting away.

Worse for the millennials, this is all happening exactly when the boomers are reinventing aging, producing a much more proactive and aggressive "army" that, unlike previous generations of senior citizens, will not sit back and accept a few crumbs.

We've already looked at some of the details of these two big sets of circumstances – the economic meltdown and the reinvention of aging – and we'll be probing them further in later chapters when we look at how some of the early battles are actually taking shape.

But what about the millennials themselves? Why are they so ill-equipped to fight off the boomers and seniors? Why, as I believe, are they bound to lose out in the battle for scarce resources? There are two main reasons.

1. The boomers have marginalized millennials demographically: There aren't enough millennials to make a difference

2. The boomers have rendered millennials powerless: The millennials are the product of a social, cultural, and educational machine that has demonstrably fostered immaturity, non-performance, and detachment from reality

Before we look at these two factors in more detail, let me clear the air by declaring a few important caveats and disclaimers and by setting a reasonable frame of reference for what follows.

First, I am emphatically *not* suggesting that the millennials are doomed for life. They may indeed mature and rebound and gain more control over their lives as they get older. So when I say "lose out," I use the phrase only in the context of the immediate struggle.

Second, as mentioned earlier, I cheerfully acknowledge that I am generalizing. I am characterizing an entire generation, and of course there are hundreds of thousands, if not millions, of individual exceptions, and even pockets of group exceptions (young high-tech entrepreneurs, for example). Point noted, and conceded, but it still doesn't undermine my thesis.

Third, I am not pretending to write an exhaustive or scholarly treatise on the millennial generation. Entire books have been, are being, and will be written on this topic, and from a wide variety of standpoints – demographic, behavioral, cultural, political, sociological. My focus here is limited strictly to the war for scarce jobs and scarce money, and to varying levels of exertion and political ability to influence (if not control) the allocation of those resources. The arguments that the millennials may have many redeeming values and qualities, that these values and qualities might have produced a very different outcome if only today's circumstances had been different, or that these values and qualities may, at some future time, yet triumph and prove to be superior to those of the boomers and seniors – these are all perfectly legitimate, and indeed compelling, topics worthy of further study and debate. But they lie outside my mandate here.

With those caveats in mind, let's dig in.

The Marginalized Millennials

The population graphs in chapter 2 told the tale in stark and uncompromising terms: The millennials are ridiculously outnumbered.

But worse: It's all the fault of the boomers.

The boomers loved sex, but didn't love big families. They believed fewer children would equal a higher quality of life. The development of the pill – the first iteration received regulatory approval in 1963 – gave the boomers an irresistible win-win. Sex became more convenient, while at the same time birth control became more reliable. What could be better?

Result? A plummeting Total Fertility Rate in Canada and the USA. The TFR for any given year is the measurement of the fertility of a hypothetical woman if she were subjected, in that one year, to all the age-specific fertility rates for ages 15 to 49. In other words, if you could compress all the different fertility rates she would come under as she aged, and apply them all in that single year, how many children would she bear?

An average of 2.1 children is considered the replacement TFR for Canada and the USA. This number – when set against the mortality rates of the two countries – would keep the population relatively stable. (The replacement rate for many Third

World countries would be as high as 3 or more because of their higher mortality rates.) Go above the replacement rate, and the population gradually skews younger, with succeeding generations being more populous than their predecessors. Go below the replacement rate, and each new generation becomes less populous than the previous one, while the population gradually skews older and older.

The baby boom, as we know, started at the end of World War II and peaked in about 1960. The birth control pill hit the market in 1963, when the oldest baby boomers were in their mid-teens. Within a few years they were in a position to be sexually active; within fewer than 10 years they were marrying and forming families.

The TFR had already started to come down from its baby boomer peaks, but by the mid-1960s the curve showed an almost straight vertical drop, crashing below the replacement level by the early 1970s. *It has never come back.*

In 1972, *New York Times* columnist Russell Baker wrote a column about how the kids – meaning the boomers – weren't having kids any more. In a humorous vein, he postulated that this was all part of a deliberate plan on their part. By having few or no kids, they would guarantee themselves a permanent majority, and thus a permanent hold on power. The boomers, in other words, were consciously and deliberately messing up as-yet-unborn future generations. Here are some excerpts from that column, written 40 years ago.

> *The kids! The kids! Remember the kids? Of course. Who could forget? They were the hit of the 60s, the agony and the glory. Already we begin to miss them ... Where have they gone, these great, exciting, infuriating kids?*
>
> *They have gone to sulk. They are poor losers, these kids. These gotta-have-it-my-way-or-I-won't-play kids. And after all we did for them, too!*

So far, a pretty good description of the boomer generation, one that, in the eyes of so many critics, holds up not too badly to this day.

Look what they're up to. Look at the birth rate. Those kids have reached the age where they ought to be having kids of their own, but they're not doing it. The birth rate is going down, down, down. The latest figures show it is now lower than at any time since records have been kept. What if ----? Dare we say it?...

What if these kids are going to quit reproducing altogether?

What if they are planning the ultimate vengeance on America? Obliteration by non-reproduction!

Having set up the wickedly hilarious thesis, Baker concedes that maybe it won't be literally zero reproduction, but then quickly resumes:

The kids must have realized, as they moved from Beatles to Stones...that if they were not careful, there would be more kids coming along to take their places. And that they, the authentic original kids...would then become, in relentlessly successive stages of Nixonic inevitability, over 30, middle-aged, and finally – the last ghastly twist of euphemism – "Senior Citizens."

It could be prevented. Yes, they would have foreseen that, these kids of ours. Oh, they were smart, those kids ... They would have grasped the point. The way to go on being the kids for the rest of their lives would have been obvious to them: cut back reproduction. Smart, eh?

Baker's razor-sharp wit disguises a more serious, and very astute, observation:

Power. That's what goes with being over 30 and middle-aged. Power. The kids, who had always wanted to run things, would now be running things. Only one thing could spoil it for them: they knew that from experience. Kids could spoil it. Their kids.

Ah, but those clever boomer kids quickly figured out the solution, Baker goes on to say. They could retain their power by making sure the coming generations would never be large enough to outnumber them. If they "cut back the birth rate to a clever point at which their own children would always remain in the minority," they could rule the roost "for years and years, maybe forever."

Tongue in cheek? Sure. The boomers in real life obviously didn't all get together in one room at one time and consciously decide to rig the deck, 40 years forward, by guaranteeing their numerical majority. But the outcome is close enough to Baker's scenario to make it almost spooky that he could have come up with it so long ago.

Here's a graph showing the trend in the TFR, for both Canada and the USA, based on data from Statistics Canada and the National Center for Health Statistics. I have superimposed some of the key events on it. Baker certainly had a crystal ball.

Total Fertility Rate, 1940-2000

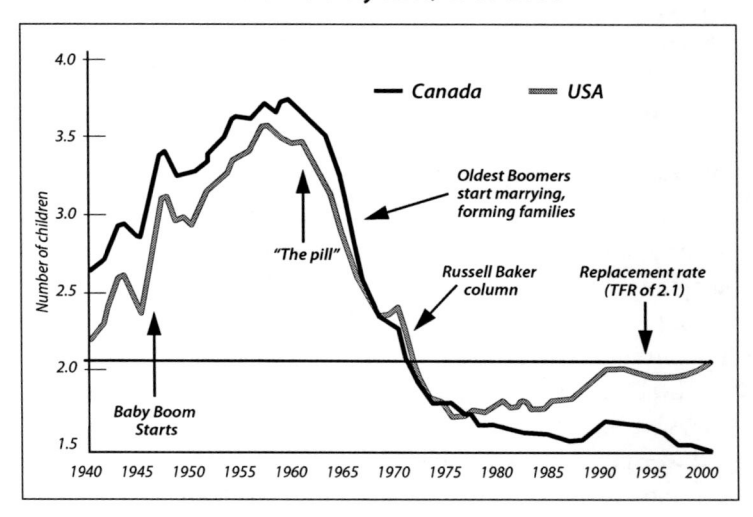

[Line graph showing Canada and USA total fertility rates from 1940 to 2000, with Number of children on the y-axis ranging from 1.5 to 4.0. Annotations include: "Baby Boom Starts" (around 1940), "The pill" (around 1960), "Oldest Boomers start marrying, forming families" (around 1965), "Russell Baker column" (around 1975), and "Replacement rate (TFR of 2.1)" (around 1990).]

It hasn't gotten any better since 2000, by the way. The Canadian TFR has bumped along in a narrow range from a high of 1.64 (2000) to a low of 1.57 (2008). The 2011 figure is 1.58. The US numbers are a bit higher, just touching the replacement rate of 2.1 only in 2008 and jockeying between 2.05, 2.06, and 2.07 the rest of the time.

As the chart makes clear, even if there wasn't the deliberate "eyes wide open" conspiracy that Baker satirized, the boomers have indeed perpetuated their own majority.

So the millennials find themselves, not just outgunned, but outgunned because of conscious attitudes and deliberate behaviors that produced much smaller families, tilting today's balance of power in favor of the boomers and seniors.

Now compound that legacy with the legacy of boomer-created debt and unaffordable future entitlements that will increasingly have to be funded by … three guesses … the millennials, and you certainly begin to understand some of the anger the millennials feel toward the older generations.

But giving birth to a smaller cohort and loading it up with future debt isn't the only Bad Thing the boomers have done to the millennials. The boomers also created (or at least it happened on their watch) a set of child-rearing values and educational theories that virtually guaranteed the millennials would be unable to cope with the challenges. Which leads us to the second big factor.

The Powerless Millennials

The millennials are the product of a boomer-created social, cultural, and educational machine that has fostered immaturity, non-performance, and detachment from reality.

Child-centered education. Helicopter parents. Grade inflation. Political correctness.

These are some of the causes that have been offered for what's wrong with the millennial generation.

I won't pretend to be able to sort it all out with any degree of certainty: I am not a psychologist or an educator, and even if I were, the nature and impact (for good or ill) of these influences are hotly contested. Did it all go bad when we stopped teaching phonics? Did the emphasis on self-esteem at all costs lead to a fatal lowering of (or banishment of) objective standards of performance? Did helicopter parents, constantly swooping down to prevent their kids from failing, inadvertently infantilize a whole generation?

You can fill a bookshelf with opinions pro and con. There are many scathing reports on the educational system and on touchy-feely parents who were less concerned about what their kids actually *knew*, or could *do*, than about preventing, at all costs, any emotional bruises. The extreme example of criticism, perhaps, is Amy Chua's best-selling *Battle Hymn of the Tiger Mother*, which derides Western-style "soft" parenting while proclaiming the value of her boot-camp, results-driven style. "What Chinese parents understand," she declares, "is that nothing is fun unless you're good at it."

There are just as many, if not more, books that argue the opposite – that the social, cultural, and educational influences on the millennials have been benign, or even highly beneficial, producing a generation whose values are of a higher order than those of work-and-money-obsessed boomers.

"Self-esteem is your child's passport to lifetime mental health and social happiness," we read on AskDr.Sears.com. "It is the foundation of a child's well-being and the key to success as an adult."

Who is Dr. Sears and does he have a clue? Okay, let's find some other authority figure. Entering "how to develop your child's self-esteem" into Google produces *6,090,000* results. By contrast, entering "the cult of self-esteem is ruining our kids" yields only 202,000.

Of course I'm just having a bit of fun here. For our purposes, what matters is not so much the weighting that is assigned to the different ingredients in the mix, but what comes out the other end.

What attitudes do the millennials bring to the party? How are they different from those of the boomers and seniors? Do the millennials' attitudes carry over into actions and behaviors that handicap either their current performance or future prospects? Do the millennials show signs of being less capable than previous generations? Is it really true, for example, that their achievements at university are below par, compared with those of previous generations? Are there other signs that the millennials are not maturing as quickly, or operating as effectively, as their parents and grandparents did?

Of course every generation is less capable, in young adulthood, than their parents or grandparents. The Pleasantville Moms and Dads who tore their hair out as their teenage daughters fainted at Elvis concerts are pushing 90 today, and those teenage daughters (and their greaser boyfriends) are now the 60-something boomers who share wistful "remember when" e-mails even as they tut-tut about the "slacker" kids and grandkids living in their basement.

But the boomers were always aggressive – and effective – in the pursuit of what they wanted. Even as they were rocking and rolling, and making out at the drive-in, and then morphing into draft-card-burners and hippies, and morphing again into money-driven Yuppies, the boomers were able to make their agenda everyone's agenda. If a boomer was less mature, at 18 or 21 or 25, than his or her parents or grandparents, it didn't mean he or she was soft or mellow or ineffective. Not only that, the boomers had the luck to born into an external environment that was much more forgiving of youthful inexperience. The economy was growing most of the time, jobs were more plentiful, and the older generations were getting out of the way on schedule.

The millennials – and it isn't their fault – have no such margin of error today.

So how do they see the world? How do they understand the problems they face? How do they see *themselves*? What are their "going-in" beliefs, perceptions, and attitudes?

In February 2010, the Pew Research Center released *Millennials: A Portrait of Generation Next*. This report was based on a national survey of 2,020 adults (with an oversampling of millennials), combined with the findings of previous surveys, census data, and other studies. It is particularly useful because it compares and contrasts millennial attitudes with those of the boomers and seniors.

The wealth of data presents a picture of a generation that is confident and optimistic, even in the face of what was already a serious recession.

A telling example is the response to the survey's question whether the respondents thought they were earning enough now, and whether they thought they would earn enough in the future.

Not surprisingly, only 31% of millennials thought they were earning enough now, compared with 46% of Generation Xers and 52% of boomers. This is logical, in that a majority of millennials would be in less-senior jobs at this point in their lives.

But when asked if they would earn enough in the future, 88% of millennials said yes, compared with 76% of Generation Xers and only 46% of boomers.

That same optimism carried over into a question about the state of the nation. When asked if they were satisfied or dissatisfied with the way things were going, 41% of the millennials said they were satisfied, compared with 36% of Generation Xers, 23% of boomers, and only 14% of seniors (or what Pew calls "the Silent Generation").

A very recent Canadian study reflects similar optimism. The *National Report Card on Youth Financial Literacy* was released by the British Columbia Securities Commission at the end of October 2011. It was based on interviews with 3,000 Canadian teenagers who had recently graduated from high school – the very youngest tranche of millennials. The findings showed a stunning disconnect from reality.

- The average respondent expected to earn $90,735 in 10 years' time – almost three times the *actual* average income of those 25 to 29 years old with post-secondary education. According to Statistics Canada (2006 data), that average income is $31,648. So the kids were off by, nothing serious, 300%

- Nearly three out of four (73%) said they expected to own a home *within the next 10 years*. Actual home ownership by those 25 to 29 years old is 42%

- 81% of the respondents said they believed they would be financially better off in life than their parents

It's true, of course, that young people have always been more upbeat than their elders, and older folks have always been grumpier, more apt to declare that the world was going to hell in a hand basket. Remember the quote I offered, on page 1, from Hesiod, almost 3,000 years ago? "I see no hope for the future of our people if they are dependent on the frivolous youth of today." So the fact that millennials are more sanguine than their more experienced elders is not, by itself, either surprising or necessarily alarming.

But the degree of error is. And the fact that those elders are considerably more alarmed makes the millennials' relative optimism dangerous ... for the millennials. Those grumpy elders, after all, account for 60% of all votes cast.

Why have the millennials been whistling past the graveyard? After all, the troubles in the economy are not exactly invisible – and there is no shortage of forecasts of long-term doom and gloom, particularly affecting that age group.

In a March 2010 article in *The Atlantic*, Don Peck offers a convincing argument that we may be entering an entire era of high unemployment, and that it may be impossible for the millennials to *ever* catch up.

"A whole generation of young adults is likely to see its life chances permanently diminished by this recession," Peck says. He cites the work of Lisa Kahn, an economist at Yale. Kahn studied the effects of recessions on lifetime earnings and found that as far out as 17 years after graduation, those who had entered the workforce "during inhospitable times" were earning 10 percent less than "those who had emerged into a more bountiful climate."

Aren't the millennials aware of any of this? What accounts for their optimism? The Pew study was released only a month before this article – and more than a year after the 2008 meltdown, when it was already painfully obvious that things were not going well.

To be fair, we should note that the millennials *are*, at last, reacting, and that much of their earlier optimism is dwindling. There has been no shortage of emotional intensity, for example, in Occupy Wall Street and its offshoots. You could argue that much of the emerging Age Rage is precisely the result of the earlier optimism, an intense rebound fueled by a sense of loss, of betrayal. The millennials are getting angry not only because things are bad, but also because it wasn't supposed to work out this way. (We'll study all this in more detail in a later chapter on the political battleground.)

But why did they believe it would work out for the better? What made them more confident in the first place?

Why could 41% of them still tell Pew – more than a year after the fall of Lehman Brothers – that the country was headed in the right direction? This was almost double the percentage of boomers who felt that way and triple the percentage of seniors who thought so.

Why could their youngest Canadian members, now just entering university, be *300% off* in their estimates of how much money they would be earning 10 years from now?

I found some interesting clues in a 2005 article in *School Administrator* magazine. In the article, Neil Howe, author of *Millennials Rising* (2000) and a prominent speaker and consultant, gives educators some tips on how to deal with millennials. He decries the negative press the millennials receive and argues effectively for a more positive outlook. Fair enough. But his observations, on how and why the millennials are the way they are, certainly don't undermine my thesis.

"These 'babies on board,'" he writes, "have been regarded as special since birth and have been more obsessed over at every age than the Gen-Xers ever were." Calling them "trophy kids," he notes that when they reached puberty in the mid-90s, "the proliferation of child-safety products and regulations paved the way for a zero-tolerance approach to hazards and misconduct in the classroom." He goes on to say:

> *From the surge in child-safety rules and devices to the post-Columbine lockdown of public schools to the hotel-style security of today's college dorm room, Americans have been tightening the security perimeters around Millennials ever since they first arrived ... Helicopter parents figure these special children always will require special care, and thus far Millennials have gone along with little resistance – unlike how Boomers would have reacted at the same age!*

So the millennials are coddled and cosseted. Bad Things are kept at a distance, if not made invisible.

In theory, a big reality check could come when they hit the university system, when they suddenly have to confront the astonishing degree of unpreparedness that the primary and high school systems have permitted (and some would say even fostered).

In practice, many of them work around it and – aided by supine faculties, powder-puff courses, and grade inflation – emerge with a degree anyway. That, plus tens of thousands of dollars of debt. And a job market that is increasingly insistent on concrete skills.

This brings me back to Ken Coates and what he calls the

entitlement generation. I was so struck by his experience and analysis of the weaknesses of the millennials that I asked if he would address a few questions specifically for this book. He was good enough to agree, and I believe you will find his observations more than a little disquieting.

Q: *Obviously you must be seeing enough of the entitlement generation student to have identified it as a general problem and not just a few isolated cases. What percentage of the students you work with would you say fall under this term?*

A: Almost all of the students have some of the characteristics of the entitlement generation. We have really worked it into the mindset of our youth. I would estimate that about half of the students have a serious entitlement problem – and truly expect the world and their lives to work out the way they want. For talented students, this is not an overwhelming problem – although it may be when they are in employment situations. For weaker students, this mindset can be really crippling.

Q: *Are your views widespread among faculty? Is this the kind of thing everybody knows but nobody wants to talk about?*

A: University faculty share the sense that the current crop of students is demanding, often ill-prepared, and less committed to their studies than we would like. Some people share the idea that they are overly entitled, but this tends to come from folks who deal directly with student complaints or appeals. Actually, I am always surprised at how little discussion there is among faculty members on student issues of this type. Student affairs folks, in contrast, discuss these issues a lot, but they tend to be more sympathetic to the students.

Q: *Is the problem widespread among universities of very high academic reputations and tough admissions, not just in universities with easier admission policies?*

A: The issue is commonplace. Arrogance among the talented is understandable, even if it is off-putting. Arrogance – which is often how entitlement shows up in students – among those of significantly lower talent is not understandable and is more disturbing. I have taught at University of Waterloo, one of the best schools in the country, and at schools with open entry policies. I have seen the same behavioral patterns at all the schools. Even weak students are told by parents and teachers that they "can be anything they want to be" – one of the most misleading and incorrect mantras in human history. In these cases, the gap between ability and aspiration is particularly large. These students should be buckling down and working three times as hard. That is rarely the approach that students take.

Q: *In your book, you write about the increasing number of high school graduates with 80% averages or more. If grade inflation is such a clear issue at the university level, dealing with all those incoming high school grads, is it also an issue at the high school level? Are those schools aware of it? Do they care? Are they doing anything about it?*

A: Grade inflation is a huge issue. Students with high grades do better than students with lower grades – so there is still predictive value. But do you believe that more than 60% of Ontario high school graduates who apply to university really warrant 80% or higher grades? The real cutoff today is around 90%, and this is where the best schools focus their recruiting attention. The most serious issue is that high grades are no assurance that the student has the expected basic skills.

Q: *The idea that high school doesn't really prepare you for university is not necessarily a new thing. But were previous generations, even though they may have been somewhat unprepared, nevertheless significantly better prepared, compared with kids today?*

A: The level of preparation – in terms of basic knowledge, fundamental skills, curiosity, and attitudes toward work – was much higher than what we see now. Students are not taught to memorize, most have little experience with really hard competition, and most are told that they are talented and of high potential (some, of course, are). We have also dismantled prestige and status from the learning process – teachers are coaches and not sources of information. There is precious little awe left among young people. They do not, as a consequence, take criticism well. Professors tend to be much more muted in their criticism than before, for fear of student complaints. It is easier and less complicated to go lightly on them.

Q: *Is this really going to be a lost generation? Is it too late to help them, and should we focus more intensely on fixing the educational system at the primary and secondary levels? Is the topic even being acknowledged in the academic world?*

A: The response to our book tells me that people are truly agitated about these issues, but no one knows what to do or is willing to do it. Politicians will not touch elementary or secondary education – the political costs of doing so are considerable. Parents who really care – a growing number – are moving their kids to private schools where these issues are taken more seriously.

We lack the determination to grapple openly with the shortcomings of our system and need to find the courage to experiment with newer, high-quality models of education. Take a look at China, Japan, Korea, Taiwan, India, Scandinavia, Israel, and other places. But I think we need to look closer to home first and look at parenting styles and expectations. Weak parenting and child-centered approaches to treating young people (particularly the self-esteem preoccupation) are leaving our children without the skills, resolve, and support needed to tackle a very challenging century.

Consult Ken Coates' book if you're interested in probing more deeply into his observations and arguments. It deals with a much wider range of topics than the problems of today's students, including university administration, funding, curriculum, tenure, and even architecture. It's a powerful view from the inside, one that is honest, intelligent, and grounded in decades of real-world experience.

Earlier in this chapter I cited Anya Kamenetz, whose book *Generation Debt* describes in excruciating detail the financial predicament faced by the millennials, particularly when it comes to the debts they've incurred in order to get a university education. She, too, agreed to answer a few questions. Most of her comments deal with the political battleground, and I'll present them in the next chapter. But on the topic of universities, I asked her about the high cost of universities and the value of all that expensive education.

> **Q:** *We're starting to read more and more about a higher education bubble – the possibility that current or prospective future students will abandon expensive college courses that don't lead to jobs, in favor of more practical, jobs-focused study. Are you seeing signs that there is, in fact, some likelihood of such a bubble? Are you seeing signs that millennials are rebelling against soft (and expensive) programs that leave them ill-equipped to compete for jobs?*

A: College tuition has grown more than any other good or service in the entire US economy since 1978. If you chart the hockey-stick path of tuition inflation, you can see that the all-but-inevitable outcome is a crash. To my mind, the main beneficiaries of that crash will be purveyors of truly low-cost, bare-bones, you-get-what-you-pay-for education, like that provided by certain online operators and community colleges. Meanwhile, prestige, full-service, exclusive higher education will continue to thrive with an increasingly international and privileged clientele, financial-aid policies notwithstanding. My hope is that a number of public universities, community colleges, and certain less-exclusive private colleges will figure out a way to innovate and provide quality, affordable higher education at the middle of the market.

Kamenetz is not alone in predicting a crash. The phrase "higher-education bubble" is being seen in more and more headlines. Although the experts (both self-styled and serious) differ on how and when, most conclude that the present levels of student loans (in the USA, over $1 trillion outstanding as of 2011) are not sustainable. Neither are tuitions.

The Economist summarized the case in the April 2011 article "Higher Education: The Next Bubble?" The article cited the views of PayPal founder Paul Thiel:

> Mr. Thiel believes that higher education fills all the criteria for a bubble: tuition costs are too high, debt loads are too onerous, and there is mounting evidence that the rewards are over-rated. Add to this the fact that politicians are doing everything they can to expand the supply of higher education (reasoning that the "jobs of the future" require college degrees), much as they did everything that they could to expand the supply

of "affordable" housing, and it is hard to see how we can escape disaster.

Thiel feels so strongly that he created a special scholarship offering 20 students $100,000 each, over two years, if they would leave school and start a company rather than enter university.

But meanwhile, back in the classroom, let me offer again the last sentence of Prof. Ken Coates' answer to my final question:

Weak parenting and child-centered approaches to treating young people (particularly the self-esteem preoccupation) are leaving our children without the skills, resolve, and support needed to tackle a very challenging century.

This is more than just an observation. More than a prediction. It's a description of what we can see is already happening – or perhaps more accurately, *not* happening – when the millennials graduate.

What is not happening is the easy, almost automatic success they were promised (or perceive they were promised). They leave university burdened by debt – staggering debt, in many cases, particularly for students in the United States – only to discover that the education for which they incurred that debt has not equipped them to compete in a brutally competitive job market. Not surprisingly, they look for someone to blame.

The angry words are flying. It's easy to think that hostilities have commenced.

Let's take a closer look.

Age Rage – and Beyond

Residence Locator | Advice Guide | Financing | Videos | Con

Health and Wellness | Relationships | Finances and Law | Leisure and Ev

You are here: Home / Finances and Law / Second Careers – Second Chances For Seniors

Second Careers – Second Chances For Seniors
SEPTEMBER 12, 2011 BY CHARTERED ACCOUNTS OF ONTARIO COMMENTS (0)

Today's Canadians are healthier and living longer. So it's probably not surprising that many are choosing to extend their work lives past the traditional age 65.

comfortlife.ca

CareerRook
Internships, part-time jobs and

HOME | RESUME | FIND JOBS | ADVICE & RESOURCES | VIDEOS

Entry Level Jobs, Internships, and Part-Time Work

1 2 3 4 5 6 7 8

Follow CareerRookie On: Follow @CareerRookie   Facebook   RSS

careerrookie.com

The Jobs Battle

*T*HE needs and wants of the boomers and seniors, and those of the millennials, are forced, by today's economic problems and scarcity of resources, into a competitive relationship. The urgency of these economic problems – serious in Canada, more serious in the USA, and becoming desperate in the EU – elevates, in the eyes of many observers, "competitive relationship" to "war."

But how real is the analogy? Is it all just a matter of inflated rhetoric? Or are the interests – and more importantly, the actions – of the boomers and seniors actually causing damage to the millennials?

We'll apply these questions to two fronts – the private sector and the public sector. On the first front, the subject of this chapter, are underfunded boomers who can't afford to retire plus seniors who have suddenly seen their retirement funds shrivel vs. just-out-of-school millennials. On the second front, to be examined in the next two chapters, are boomers and seniors fighting to protect pensions and health-care entitlements vs. millennials looking for more funding for education and relief from crippling student loans.

The battle for jobs is taking place in the teeth of a stalled-out economy, one in which employers are in no rush to hire.

The battle for public funds is taking place at a time when

governments, which never had enough revenue to satisfy everyone's claims, are suddenly finding themselves unable to borrow the money, either.

And, yes, on both battlefields, we are already starting to hear the gunfire.

Before 2008

The first important observation is that, even without the economic meltdown that started at the end of 2008, *the boomers and seniors were already not retiring on schedule*. As we outlined in chapter 5, there are three reasons:

- Attitude: The reinvention of aging, led by the boomers, indicating a desire and determination to keep active, keep vital, stay in the game as long as possible

- Longevity: A retirement plan that may have been enough for a time when people only lived into their 70s isn't enough today. More money is needed, making it necessary for people to work longer

- Underfunding: Most boomers don't even have a retirement plan that would have been okay in years past; they have much less. In Canada, only 20% have retirement savings of $250,000 or more, and a third have less than $100,000; in the USA, boomers over age 55 have saved an average of less than $50,000, and boomers under age 55 have saved an average of less than $30,000

As a result, people have been staying in the workforce longer. As Statistics Canada reports, there was a trend toward earlier retirement in the 1980s and early 1990s, "prompted by high public-sector deficits and downsizing of private-sector organizations." But in the late 1990s the trend reversed itself. This graphic shows the employment rate for Canadians over the age of 55.

Employment and Retirement Trends, Canadians 55+

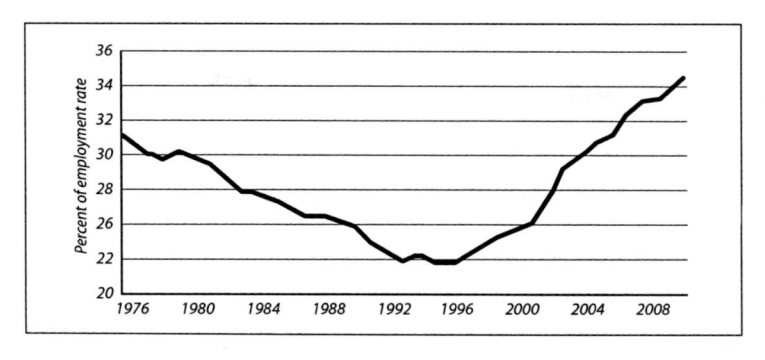

Going forward, Statistics Canada sees a continuation of the trend, "given that Boomers are more highly educated" and "the coverage rate of defined-benefit pension plans is on a downward trend." Statistics Canada also notes that "work is becoming less physically demanding due to technological advances." As well, the trend may have been "amplified by the recent recession and financial crisis, as well as the debt load of workers nearing retirement. These factors may have already prompted a number of workers to postpone their retirement."

The US has experienced the same trends. The participation rate of older workers decreased, then bottomed out in the late 1990s, then started to climb. Here is a graph from the US Department of Labor.

Labor Force Participation Rate, US 65+

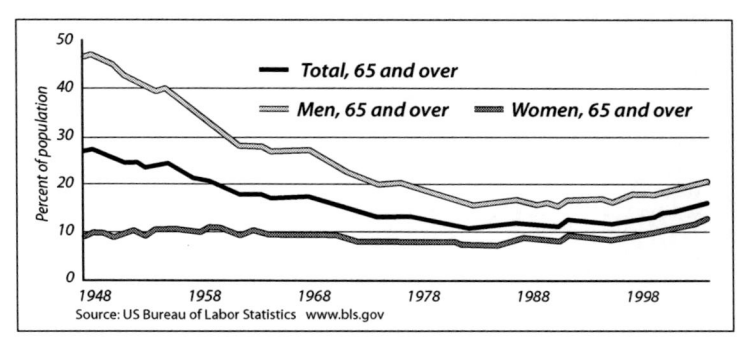

Source: US Bureau of Labor Statistics www.bls.gov

In this case, the age group under study is 65-plus, compared with the Canadian figures, which are based on people 55-plus, but the pattern is basically the same.

Between 1977 and 2007, there was a 59% increase in the number of workers age 16 and up, but a 101% increase in the number of workers age 65 and up. There was also a 172% increase in the number of workers age 75 and up. This means that even if the millennials weren't hitting a tight job market, they were always going to be hitting a job market with a lot of older workers not in any hurry to leave.

This demonstrates that the combination of attitude and need that keeps so many boomers and seniors from retiring on schedule is not a temporary, or transitory, phenomenon brought on by the economic crunch that started in 2008. The phenomenon started a decade before and will continue even if the economy recovers and hiring rebounds. Boomers will continue to work longer, if for no other reason than that they will continue to live longer … and longer … and longer …

It's also important to observe that the war for jobs didn't start out as us-against-them. The aging of the workplace began when there was much less unemployment. Yes, boomers and seniors were staying in the workforce longer because of their own needs, but they were just as happy to see younger workers' needs met at the same time. If there were jobs for all, no problem.

And there *were* jobs for all. Here, from Statistics Canada, is the Canadian unemployment rate, by age, to the end of 2007.

Unemployment Rate in Canada 65+

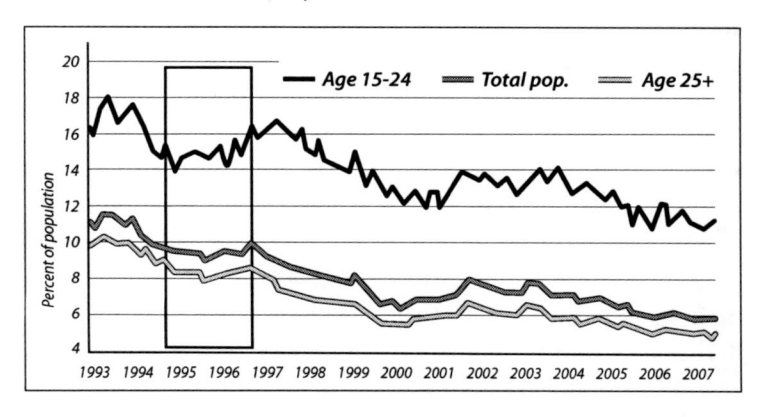

The rectangle in the mid-to-late 1990s represents the period when the previous trend toward earlier retirement began to reverse itself, when boomers and seniors started delaying retirement and staying in the workforce longer. As you can see, the trend put no damper on the employment of other age groups. Unemployment rates trended downward. The economy was generally strong. The presence of a higher number of older workers did not inhibit the employability of younger workers.

Unemployment data that I was able to find for the USA cover a different date range, but the age breakdown is more detailed.

US Unemployment by Age Group

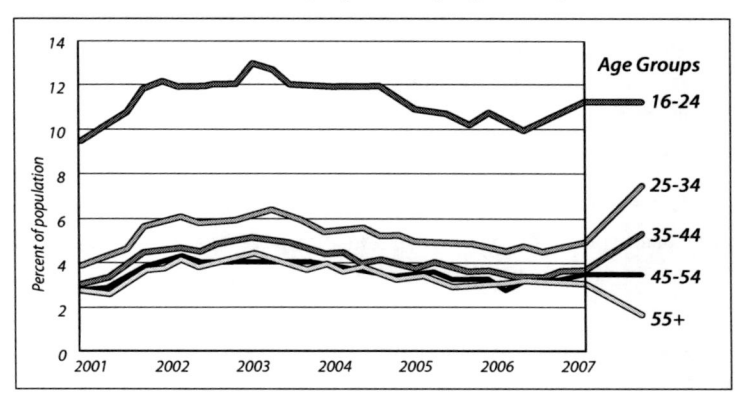

As in Canada, the fact that more people were delaying retirement and staying in the workforce longer did not automatically cause an increase in unemployment rates for younger workers.

In fact, before the economic meltdown, the biggest problem seen concerning the presence of older workers was the challenge of managing a more age-diverse workforce. A number of business and management books appeared in the early 2000s to deal with this issue.

A good example was *When Generations Collide*, written by Lynne C. Lancaster and David Stillman, published in 2002. The book's subtitle summarizes the book nicely: *Who They Are. Why They Clash. How to Solve the Generational Puzzle at Work*. While acknowledging that "economic slowdowns are likely to make the job market tighter," the authors are more worried about talent shortages.

> *There's a talent war out there. Because Generation X is just little over half the size of the Baby Boom, regardless of what happens with the economy, fewer workers will be available in the age group that's poised to move into the management ranks. At the same time, a large number of Boomers will become eligible to retire over the next few years, leaving a leadership gap at the upper echelons of organizations. Many Traditionalists will be able to afford to leave the work world at relatively young ages, and the bulk of the Millennials are still a decade or two away from filling management gaps. The result is that businesses will have to fight harder to recruit and retain the best and brightest employees.*

There's not an unreasonable word in this, and the authors (Lancaster is a baby boomer, and Stillman a Gen Xer) can hardly be faulted for not being able to see beyond 2002 to the wreckage of 2008.

What's more, the book does deal with an important issue that will endure. The workforce that the baby boomers joined when they were coming into adulthood might have had a 40-year spread, between a 20-something entry-level boomer and a 60-something VP or CEO. But the bulk of the workforce would have occupied a 25- to 30-year spread, at most. In the future, that spread could be 50 years or more, especially if a meaningful number of workers may be part-time or contract employees in their 70s or even 80s. (The latter is increasingly likely as our knowledge economy puts a premium on intellectual, rather than physical, skills and experience.)

How *do* you manage such a workforce, one with such a wide range of attitudes and experiences? The authors present valuable insights and advice. It's important for me to say this because I don't want you to think I'm cherry-picking a few paragraphs and pouncing with an unfair "aha!" just because the writers didn't have a crystal ball.

The initial reaction to the aging of the workforce, then, was not one of alarm – and certainly not one that saw the situation as a threat to the employment prospects of the younger generations. The war, to the extent there was one (and Lancaster and Stillman's book does talk about "battle" and "conflict" and "ClashPoints"), was within the workplace itself, between groups who were by definition *employed*, and whose contrasting attitudes required only a little finessing, through management skills that could be learned.

After 2008

The effect on unemployment of the economic meltdown in 2008 was immediate and dramatic.

Here's Canada, in an extension of the unemployment graph presented above.

Canadian Unemployment Rate to 2011

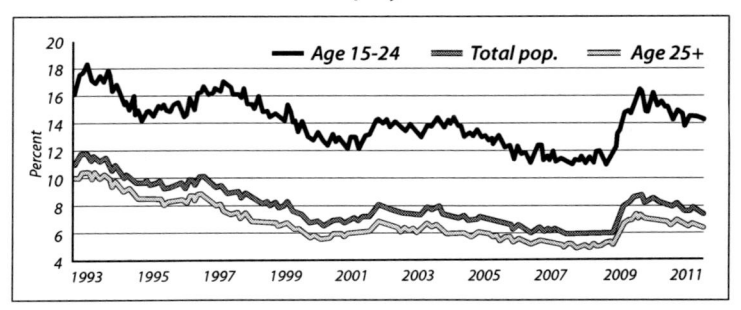

Note that the younger workers' rate jumps more than the older workers. And consider the following more detailed breakdown of how things stood, per Statistics Canada, by the end of 2010.

Canadian Unemployment by Age Group 2010

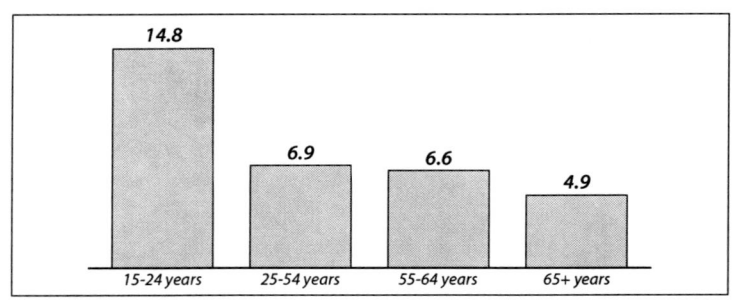

Age Group	Rate
15-24 years	14.8
25-54 years	6.9
55-64 years	6.6
65+ years	4.9

The unemployment rate for the youngest age group is 14.8%, while it's just less than 7% for boomers and only 4.9% for seniors who are still in the labor force.

The numbers from the USA are much worse. Again, let's extend the earlier unemployment data to 2008 and beyond.

USA Unemployment Rate by Age Groups to 2011

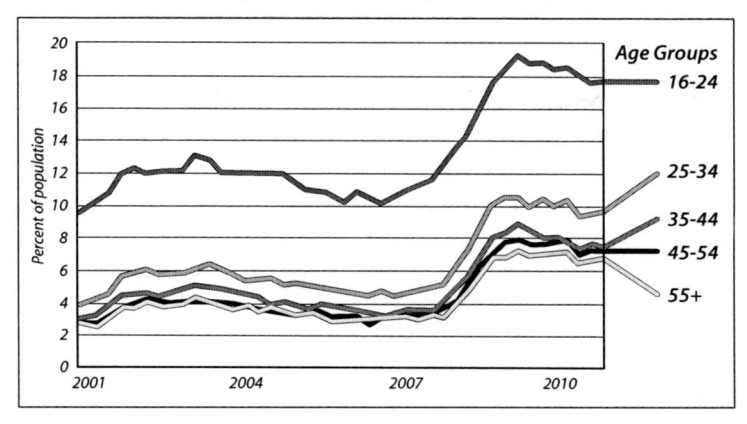

(Chart: Percent of population, 2001–2010, showing unemployment rates for age groups 16-24, 25-34, 35-44, 45-54, 55+)

The unemployment rate for the 16- to 24-year-old group *almost doubles* – from 10% in mid-2007 to 19% by mid-2009 – before falling back to just 18% in the third quarter of 2011, just weeks before this was written. The unemployment rate among those ages 25 to 34 *more than doubles* – from about 5% entering 2008 to over 10% by mid-2009 – before dropping to just under 10% by late 2011.

Not that the boomers and seniors are having a picnic, either. The unemployment rate among the younger boomers (ages 45 to 54) almost doubles, from under 4% heading into 2008 to almost 8% heading into 2010, while the combined rate for older boomers and seniors has a similar jump, from under 4% to almost 7%, over the same period.

Everyone's scratching and clawing now. But does this mean that boomers and seniors are actually competing for the same jobs as millennials? Are they really taking jobs away from the younger group?

The short answer is, "Not always, of course." Obviously there isn't an automatic reciprocal relationship between each employed boomer or senior and each unemployed millennial. Thousands of individual millennials are being hired, even in this terrible economy; thousands of individual boomers and seniors are losing their jobs. And older workers often find it more difficult to get a new job than younger workers do.

A Generational Competition for Jobs

That said, the factors behind the dampening of job prospects for younger workers are easy to see.

The first factor is delayed retirement. If boomers or seniors were staying in the workforce longer when times were good, they're hanging on even more tenaciously today. If "clogging the pipeline" was no more than an irritant when jobs were relatively plentiful, today it's a huge issue between just-out-of-university millennials and that all-important entry-level position.

"The Boomers are staying in the system longer, and that's clogging the system," says Mason Jackson, president of Workforce One, a federally funded agency helping the unemployed in Florida's Broward County. He was quoted in a *New York Times* article of March 20, 2009, "Young and Old Are Facing Off for Jobs." The article notes:

> *Millions of older Americans have delayed retirement because of plummeting 40lks, soaring health costs, a sense that Social Security benefits alone are too little to live on or all of the above. This delay, economists say, has made it harder for millions of young workers to climb onto the first rung or two of the career ladder, especially since many employers favor hiring applicants with a track record.*

But delayed retirement is only one factor causing competition. Another is the fact that a significant number of out-of-work boomers and seniors are being forced to come out of retirement to replace at least part of their devastated retirement nest eggs. In the USA, it's been estimated that the economic meltdown wiped out over $2 trillion in retirement savings – and as of 2012 we're not rebounding with any vigor. The need for more cash to fund greater longevity – a new permanent factor even in boom times – is now made even more urgent by the disappearance of so much cash from retirement nest eggs.

So now the millennials face a double squeeze, between boomers and seniors who are already employed and aren't going anywhere, thank you, and boomers and seniors who have either lost their jobs or have to get back into the workforce to replenish (at least partially) their lost retirement savings (or in the case of boomers, savings they never had in the first place and suddenly realize they need). The result? More head-to-head competition for scarce vacancies.

The article goes on to say: "Along the ocean beaches and the Intracoastal Waterway here, retirees in condominiums have long coexisted with a much younger generation, but in the depressed job market, tensions have swelled as each group complains that employers improperly favor the other."

This article isn't a one-off, either. Descriptions of generation-against-generation competition, and even the use of terms such as "battle" or "war," are becoming more and more commonplace in the media.

"Younger and Older Bay State Workers Compete in a Tough Economy" is the headline of a July 23, 2011, article on the website of Boston's National Public Radio affiliate. "Bay State baby boomers and their children share many traits," the article notes. "They're independent. Ambitious. Motivated. They're also competing – sometimes with each other – for jobs." The article makes the observation – in the context of a particular state, but it is an observation that should be familiar to us by now – that "a growing number of Massachusetts employees are working past traditional retirement age." As a result, "they are reducing opportunities for younger workers who are also facing the most difficult job market in a generation." The article concludes that "this trend has produced a job squeeze that's strangling two generations. Older workers can't retire. Younger workers can't begin building their futures."

On BusinessInsider.com, in September 2011, Joe Weisenthal comments on a Wells Fargo chart showing the participation rate of different age groups in the labor force. "This may be the most striking chart there is when it comes to changes in the labor market," he writes. "Since 2001, the participation rate for older workers has grown rapidly, as people hold on to their jobs longer, pushing retirement off further into the future. Conversely, younger generations have dropped out of the work force *en masse*."

All perfectly true, and reasonable, and the chart certainly adds some interesting depth to the other exhibits I have presented above.

Participation Rate Change

By Age Cohort, Percentage Point Change Since January 2002

Age Groups
- 65+: Aug.@+4.5
- 55+: Aug.@+2.8
- 25-54: Aug.@-2.0
- 20-24: Aug.@-6.2
- 16-19: Aug.@-14.2

But the title of the article – "The War Between Young People and Old People for Jobs" – is anything but measured.

Given the trend lines in the chart, it seems the older generations are winning. Below the age of 54, every age group's participation rate has declined since 2002. Only the 55-plus and 65-plus age breaks show an increase in labor force participation.

"When Young and Old Compete for Jobs, Who Wins?"

asks an August 2010 article by Maria Hanson on JobsDb.com. Hanson concludes that it's often the older workers who come out on top. "Figures from the Bureau of Labor Statistics show that younger workers are getting the ax while older workers are more likely to keep their jobs," she notes. "And many jobs that would traditionally go to younger, less-experienced workers are getting swept up by seniors who are coming out of retirement because their nest eggs have disappeared."

As an interesting side note, in 2009, McDonald's in the UK urged employers to hire a larger number of older workers. This was on the heels of a study of 400 McDonald's restaurants by Lancaster University Management School, which found that restaurants that had hired staff over age 60 had experienced a 20% increase in customer satisfaction. According to the study, 47% of the McDonald's managers said they felt older workers did more to provide good service, 69% of them thought older workers connected better with customers, and 44% thought older workers brought worthwhile mentoring skills that would help younger employees.

The same theme is sounded in a March 2011 article on CNN Money, "A Tough Market for Teens, Thanks to Grandpa." Once again, it's those nasty geezers taking jobs away from Junior.

"Today, grandpa is more likely to earn a paycheck than his grandson," says the author of the article, Nin-Hai Tseng. "Baby boomers have either stayed at their jobs longer, or taken lower-skills jobs ordinarily filled by younger workers, for various reasons that include the plunge in stock prices following the financial crisis and the recession."

The article quotes Andrew Sum, an economics professor and director of Center for Labor Market Studies at Northeastern University in Boston: "A lot of the jobs older people have taken would have gone to teenagers a decade ago." Sum cites jobs in retail stores and fast-food outlets and observes that employers are starting to favor older workers with "soft skills," such as "showing up on time, taking orders and so forth."

How unfair. Drat those hard-working geezers.

Even when workers from both generations are employed in the same place, employers are starting to squeeze the younger workers. The *New York Times* reported, in September 2011, that Chrysler was introducing a two-tier pay system under which new young recruits would be paid about half the hourly rate of older workers doing the same job. "The arrival of vastly different wage rates in auto factories," the *Times* observed, "is a seminal event in an industry long influenced by a powerful union devoted to equal pay regardless of seniority."

Walter Russell Mead, the distinguished academic and author, comments on the *Times* piece in a September 13, 2011, article on the blog of *The American Interest*. In his article, entitled "The War Against the Young: Detroit Edition," Mead indicates that the deal is "just another battlefield in the war against the young." Mead, who, I should note, turns 60 in 2012, continues:

> *The reality is that American auto workers are not productive enough (and Detroit's management is not creative enough) to justify their high wages ... That's sad but it's a fact of life. But when it comes to adjustments, the union movement and the older generation at large makes sure that the pain falls on the young rather than spreading it around.*

Mead goes on to deplore the fact that younger workers' taxes fund a level of health care for today's seniors that will no longer be affordable when the youngsters become seniors themselves. "Will America's young people realize they are being systematically scammed and organize to stop it," he asks, "or will the older generations continue to pull the wool over those adorable little eyes?"

It's a reasonable question, one we'll look at more closely in the next two chapters, in which we survey the political battlefield.

But in the meantime, note that less than two weeks after

Mead wrote his comments, the United Auto Workers accepted – along with other painful cost-cutting measures – the same two-tier kind of structure in their contract with General Motors.

Given the severity of the American downturn, it is perhaps not surprising to see such dramatic headlines and heated language. Does the same apply in Canada, where the numbers haven't been nearly as bad?

Maclean's magazine was on this as early as January 2009, with the provocative piece "Dude, Where's My Job?" by Lianne George, co-author of *The Ego Boom: Why the World Really Does Revolve Around You*. The subtitle of the article is, "What Happens When the Most Entitled Generation Ever Hits a Recession," and the author is blunt and unsparing in contrasting the pre-recession expectations of the millennials with the post-recession reality that suddenly confronted them.

> *It was only 18 months ago that the* Wall Street Journal *ran an article outlining the lavish demands of a new generation of workers, known collectively as Gen Y or Millennials or Net Gen. At the time, the thinking was that this group – ages 30 and under – had employers over a barrel.*

And with good reason. There was an expected wave of boomer retirement that would create a scarcity of job talent. What's more, the emerging generation of workers, being so Internet savvy, "were believed to possess magical and mysterious tech skills that would prove invaluable in the workplace of the future." Not surprisingly, the millennials expected a lot.

> *Not only did they want fun, fulfilling work, with flexible hours, good salaries, and ample vacation, they wanted to be celebrated, too. Literally, feted. Savvy employers had taken to embracing measures like prize packages for a job well done, "public displays of appreciation," and,*

in the case of one manufacturer in Texas, retaining a "celebration assistant" in charge of helium balloons and confetti.

But then reality hit, in the form of the worst job market in 30 years. "Almost as soon as they began for this cohort," writes George, "it would appear its halcyon days are over."

The article goes on to detail some of the carnage – and this was at the start of 2009, remember, when the worst was yet to come – and note a few of the additional forces that were adding to the problems ("Suddenly, many of those retiring boomers can't afford to retire"). Then it explains why the millennials are so ill-equipped: "Well-intentioned attempts to make this generation feel good about itself have, in fact, left them poorly prepared to weather a tough economic storm."

George cites factors like the self-esteem craze and the watering-down of competition and marking standards. "It only makes sense that the environment in which they were raised would inform what they expected from a job – namely, flexibility, authority, instant respect and continuous affirmation."

George does end on a note of optimism, pointing out the potential advantage to millennials and prospective employers that the millennials' demands are not all based on money. To some degree, she notes, "employers may be able to substitute applause for hard currency and still keep young employees perfectly happy, a potential boon in a cash-strapped economy."

It's an astute observation, but it matters only if the millennials are being hired in the first place. As the economy gets tougher, though, the number of attractive jobs shrinks and more millennials are forced to accept often-menial jobs outside their fields of study – if they can find even those. Having McDonald's celebrate your birthday – no offence to McDonald's – may not be quite what you had in mind when you were earning that BA in Gender Studies. (And let's not forget those seniors applying to McDonald's, either.)

Fast-forward two years, and the mood isn't any better. Here is Vanessa Lu, writing in the *Toronto Star* on October 3, 2011, under the headline "Young, Educated and Unemployed."

> *Young people have always struggled to find work, but in difficult economic times it becomes more pronounced. The barriers pile up. Mandatory retirement has been eliminated, baby boomers are choosing to hang on to their jobs, and workers who have been laid off are competing with new graduates for a smaller pool of jobs.*

Not even two weeks later, here is Carol Goar, also in the *Toronto Star*. This time, the headline is more inflammatory: "Selfish Boomers or Pushy Kids?" (Note that she uses the term Generation Y, the other name for millennials.)

> *The subject is too divisive to talk about. Politicians won't touch it; business leaders seldom mention it; even within families, it is awkward.*
>
> *The baby boom generation won't let go. The 45-to-65 year old cohort that stretched the school system, the universities, the workforce and the housing market is now firmly entrenched atop the employment hierarchy. Generation X (30- to 40-year-olds) can't move up. Generation Y (20- to 30-year-olds) can't get stable work, rent an apartment or start a family.*

Goar goes on to argue that this picture is simplistic: The so-called selfish "job blockers" are often supporting grown children and grandchildren, she says, while the young job seekers are only expecting what their education taught them to expect.

Here's Tim Shufelt in a *Financial Post* article – also in October 2011 – "Generation Unlucky: From Boom to Gloom."

> *Landing that first career position has never been easy. But the labour force's youngest cohort seems to have some legitimate grievances.*

> *Older workers are clinging to their jobs longer, eating up available salary and squeezing the job market from the top. That's exacerbating competition for junior vacancies, which high youth unemployment indicates are already in short supply.*

Right. Those dirty rotten older workers again.

And if you think their stubborn presence in the workforce is bad now, just wait. According to a US survey released by Wells Fargo & Co. in November 2011, 25% of respondents (of all ages) said they expected to have to work *at least until age 80* because they would not have enough money to retire comfortably before then. And even those who expected to be able to retire earlier than that said they would likely keep working anyway – either to pay for the extras they wanted or needed to maintain their lifestyle, or simply because they wanted to.

But according to Shufelt the old folks are doing a lot worse than merely "eating up available salary and squeezing the job market from the top."

> *When boomers eventually do leave their jobs en masse, the capacity of the workforce to finance those retirements will be tested. And the dwindling of defined-benefit pension plans will make it more difficult for Millennials to save for their own retirements, which can't even begin until they reconcile their record high student debt loads.*

Shufelt points the finger at boomers, who, following "a stretch of relative economic prosperity," are "committing younger generations to a fate of austerity and stagnancy – an intergenerational transfer dubbed 'fiscal child abuse' by one pundit."

Fiscal child abuse, no less. Isn't that just exquisite?

The Millennials Respond

Most of the hue and cry, of course, comes not from journalists or commentators but from the millennials themselves. Thus Age Rage. But before looking at what they're feeling and saying – plus some spirited pushback from the boomers – let's take a brief look at some of the ways the generations are responding to the jobs crisis.

Both generations are equally availing themselves of traditional job-finding institutions – government and private employment agencies, job fairs, and Internet job sites. The millennials are probably using the Internet more effectively than are boomers and seniors, and there are a number of specialty websites focusing on the unique needs and problems of first-time job seekers.

A good example is Career Rookie, which offers advice on how to get a job and an extensive listing of internships, part-time jobs, and other entry-level paths to a career. The tone its home page is very realistic, and it's particularly interesting to note the realization that unpaid internships may be a feasible way of getting into the workforce.

"Unpaid internships are on the rise as the economy continues its sluggish pace following the financial crisis," says a report on TheTicker.com in August 2011. "More and more students are faced with a difficult choice between internship experience and a paid job. Internships have grown to be an important element within the labor market. Internships are important to equip college students with the necessary tools to demand greater job offerings and higher starting salaries."

Maybe, but internships can also be seen as exploitation – months of free labor producing little or no bankable experience.

Indeed, the article goes on to quote Ross Perlin, author of *Intern Nation: How to Earn Nothing and Learn Little in the Brave New Economy*. "If you're asked by a prospective employer about the kind of salary you're looking for and what you've made in the past," he says, "it certainly raises questions to say you've worked a lot and never been paid. Many employers are now wary of CVs packed with vague-sounding internships, and pay is the clearest way to show that you performed valued, important work during your internship."

Internships also create issues such as fair employment practices, labor codes, and other regulations. In the UK, angry interns launched a website to expose companies they claimed were using internships as a way of getting lots of free work for no training or advancement. Those named include a large employment agency. Government legal advisors have warned that tens of thousands of unpaid interns may be entitled to compensation and that companies may be in breach of minimum wage laws.

Notwithstanding all this, it's been estimated that over 80% of internships are unpaid.

University graduates, particularly in science and technology fields where there are strong professional networks to plug into, are also using business-oriented websites such as LinkedIn. There's also widespread use of social media to try to turn up leads, generate referrals, and keep up to date on opportunities.

It's important to note all of these activities. It would be unfair to suggest that the millennials are, as a generation, calmly accepting their fate and doing little or nothing to find employment. They may have been stunned by what they found when they hit the job market – and, as I will show, they display plenty of Age Rage at their cruel fate and those who they believe have brought it upon them – but it doesn't mean they are all idly standing by. Take even a cursory look at youth-oriented job boards, discussion forums, and blogs and you see story after story of hundreds of résumés sent, hundreds of doors knocked on, and still no job.

Older Workers Get Creative

At the other end of the age spectrum, the boomers and seniors are also working hard to find – or keep – employment. They have both a built-in advantage and a built-in disadvantage.

The disadvantage is easy enough to name – age. Despite some laws against age discrimination in the workplace, it is obvious that it will usually be much harder for unemployed people in their 60s to find a job than for unemployed people in their 20s. There's a smaller range of jobs that would be suitable for an older worker, and many employers would be concerned, not unreasonably, about investing in training a worker who has fewer years of future employment potential.

As of fall 2011, the average length of unemployment in the USA for job seekers over the age of 55 was 52.4 weeks, compared with 37.4 weeks for those younger.

But older workers have advantages, too. I'm not sure they offset the disadvantages by a wide enough margin to produce a happy outcome for every boomer or senior in this very tough job market. I'm certainly not trying to portray a scenario in which the ultra-effective older workers are being hired in droves while the ineffective millennials are being rejected. In fact, I'm even happy to concede that the biggest negative impact boomers and seniors are exerting on the job prospects of millennials comes not from their effectiveness but simply from their numbers. The sheer tonnage of so many of them either delaying retirement or trying to get back into the workforce means that even if a significant percentage of them are unsuccessful, the remainder exerts a decisive drag on the millennials' potential for success.

But the boomers and seniors do bring more than numbers.

Their first advantage is the flip side of their disadvantage: Age means experience, and, perhaps just as importantly, it means that wider job-finding networks have been built – personal contacts, professional and trade associations, social organizations. This not a critique of the millennials, of course; it is a simple statement of reality.

Their second advantage is one of attitude, particularly on the part of boomers, who are reinventing every aspect of aging. As we have seen, they have a determination to act younger than their chronological age – to continue to be active, aggressive, and in control of their own destinies. Given this mindset, it is relatively easier for them to adapt – to "reinvent" who they are and what they can do; to change, without blinking, the traditional definitions of retirement; to redefine their entire approach to work and leisure.

As a result, we find the older generations not just using the traditional job-hunting channels but proactively creating new ones.

For example, job fairs sponsored by the AARP, formerly known as the American Association of Retired Persons. With over 30 million members, AARP is the largest association for boomers and seniors in the USA. In spring 2010 it announced it would be sponsoring 48 career fairs for older workers in 19 states with high levels of unemployment.

The "Helping Experience Work@50+" events are free and will offer workshops on promoting yourself at 50+, emphasizing tips and techniques for success in a competitive job market. Career counseling will be available to assist job seekers in assessing their skills to identify the best employment opportunities. Participants will also have the chance to interact with employers with job openings, as well as access to an Internet cafe where they can post resumes. AARP will sponsor booths at each event, promoting free online resources that provide important tips and tools to help older workers succeed in their job search.

There's nothing revolutionary about any of these support

vehicles, except that they are now being deployed on behalf of older workers ... even retirees.

The AARP website quotes Deborah Russell, AARP Director of Workforce Issues, as saying the organization "recognizes that millions of older Americans are trying to stay employed or get back on the job for a variety of reasons. Older workers continue to face difficult challenges in today's economic downturn. Many retirees have been forced back into the job market due to decimated retirement nest eggs and skyrocketing health care costs."

Rise of the BoomerPreneur

Boomers and seniors are also actively pursuing self-employment. AllBusiness.com in June 2010 reported a trend of seniors buying franchises.

> Think it's too late to start a business? Think again. It's never too late. Indeed, the fact that entrepreneurship is even alive and kicking these days is largely thanks to America's seniors. According to a 2009 report by the Ewing Marion Kauffman Foundation, in every single year from 1996 to 2007, Americans between the ages of 55 and 64 had a higher rate of entrepreneurial activity than those aged 20 to 34. The report even goes so far as to predict that the United States is on the cusp of an entrepreneurship boom and that seniors will be driving the movement.

The article quotes Victoria Conte, vice president of operations for Matchpoint Franchise Consulting Network: "We have definitely noticed more seniors investigating and investing in franchises. We are an aging society, and the older population is now more active. Seniors also have the desire and need to generate additional retirement income due to economic factors."

Her views are echoed by Art Koff, founder of RetiredBrains. com: "We have had substantial traffic to our 'Start Your Own

Business' pages as many older job seekers have given up on finding employment and are looking for other ways to make money in order to live the lifestyle they had hoped to live during their retirement years."

Jeff Bevis, founder and president of First Light Home Care, is also quoted in the article, with an endorsement from the franchisors' point of view:

> *"Not only are seniors attracted to franchise opportunities,"* he says, *"but they also make excellent franchise candidates. Older franchisees have a wisdom in their years. They often better understand how to work effectively with others. They often have deep experience building teams, possess a successful track record managing people, and have weathered the ups and down of economic cycles. They are resilient. They bring their experience in knowing they do not have all the answers. They see and often value more quickly the benefits of following a system while blending their own learning to make their businesses even better."*

These same trends are evident in Canada.

"Their careers will not come to a full stop," says Patricia Lovett-Reid, financial planning expert and best-selling author, talking about the boomers in a column on MSNMoney.com in January 2011. "Instead, they'll pursue consultancies or part-time opportunities. Of course, this will supplement retirement income. Perhaps more importantly for boomers, it will continue to provide a sense of professional fulfillment."

According to an August 2011 report from the BMO Retirement Institute, the number of self-employed Canadians 55 years and older *doubled* between 1990 and 2008. "Canadian Boomers will be making the most of their downtime," says the report, "with millions expected to launch 'semi-retirement' businesses as their careers wind down." BMO calls them BoomerPreneurs – and so do many others.

boomerpreneur

---If you're a Baby Boomer who's NOT INTERESTED in spending the second or third half of your life rocking on your proverbial front porch -- if, instead, you'd rather climb rocks or take in a rock concert -- then you need to take a few minutes to read this ... all the way to the end. What I'm about to share has the potential to rock your world and prevent you from hitting rock bottom!

"Finally, a Foolproof, Connect-the-Dots, Step-by-Step, Paint-by-Number System that's Designed to Take You By the Hand and Show You How to Leverage Your Life Experience into Financia

Anne L. Holmes, APR

Friday, February 10, 2012

Dear Friend,

I know exactly what's going on in your head. As a Baby 1946 and 1964, you've noticed that the world is start nothings to you about preparing for old age. You ge insurance, invitations to seminars about LASIK and lipo how much you ought to have saved if you want to retire laxatives, little blue pills, denture cleaners, power whee pain and muscle aches.

Problem is, you're not at all ready to start winding d really see that happening for at least a couple more thinking about launching that lifelong dream you've beer about starting your own business and being your own b the leap to owning your own business.

While friends or family fret over the late-in-life timing of you know you've deferred your vision long enough. the new 50" so you've got lots of active life ahead of you

www. boomerpreneur.com

www.amazon.com/BoomerPreneurs-Boomers-Start-Their-Business/dp/0972874836

BoomerPreneurs
How Baby Boomers Can Start Their Own Business, Make Money and Enjoy Life

M. B. IZARD

BOOMER Café ...it's your place

HOME   PAST STORIES   ABOUT BOOMERCAFÉ™   CONTACT   STORY SUBMISSIONS

You are here: Home » Baby Boomers » Support All Boomerpreneurs

Support All Boomerpreneurs
Cate | May 7, 2010 | 6 Comments

We have long since shown the world that Baby Boomers are inventive, inventive, and innovative. So when times get tough, what do we do? In an economy where jobs are tight and boomers can be at a disadvantage, many have started their own businesses. Shelly Soriba writes that in our own self-interest, we should support these Boomerpreneurs.

As the largest generation, it comes as no surprise that there are millions of Boomer-owned and operated businesses. While it is vital that we support all of our local businesses, there are additional reasons to support Boomer owned businesses. Especially now.

The current economic downturn has been especially hard on Boomers. Those who have been down-sized, right-sized, or otherwise unemployed often see little in the way of employment opportunities as millions of people fight for the few available jobs. Boomer unemployment rates and the length of time it takes to land a new job have never been higher. And no one really knows how many Boomers have given up and stopped looking for work.

While the job market is weak for all those on the outside looking in, we often face an additional obstacle: ageism. It doesn't take many clicks of your mouse to find bloggers, writers, and others who blame Boomers for just about everything that ails our country today. Some admonish us for not retiring from the workforce so more jobs will be available for younger workers. Others rant that our collective retirement will suck the economy dry as we collect Social Security and receive Medicare benefits without contributing to society.

Popular   Recent   Comments   Archives

› Baby boomers witness the most enduring quality of the 21st century
› Baby Boomers Bouncing Back from Injuries
› Where are the cheapest places to retire in the U.S.?
› Ads targeting baby boomers rule at Super Bowl
› Tom Brokaw ... You Missed Something

Subscribe for BoomerCafé™ Updates

Enter your email address below to receive updates each time we publish new content

Alltop Baby Boomer News

boomercafe.com

The topic certainly draws strong and steady reader interest on the largest website in the ZoomerMedia portfolio, <www.50Plus.com> (full disclosure: The editor, Cynthia Ross Cravit, is my wife). The website has an entire section devoted to the workplace, plus a jobs board powered by CareerBuilder Canada.

In addition to benefitting from advice to be found in articles and columns, boomers and seniors can tap into an emerging mini-industry of conferences, training programs, workshops, and even specialized networking software.

Michael Morris is a former fashion industry executive, who, in his 60s, found it difficult to get a "traditional" job – that is, working for someone else. "Boomers around the globe are struggling with the same problem of how to regain their financial independence and self-esteem," he said in a November 2011 interview with Jonathan Chevreau of the *National Post*. So he created a consulting company, built around the website socialstrategygroup.com, which links talented boomers with companies that could benefit from their experience on a short- to medium-term project basis. He is also developing a new website, <www.boomerscloud.com>, that accelerates the process.

Michael Morris represents what will become an increasingly powerful force in the market – savvy boomers converting their knowledge and experience into part-time, consulting, project-based income, and, in so doing, influencing more and more companies to understand and appreciate the value of older workers. This is being talked and written about more and more in the HR world, Morris told me in an e-mail exchange, but he believes too many companies are still missing the boat by not appreciating the value boomers and seniors can bring – value that can translate into significant improvements to a company's competitive position.

One very influential thinker in this area is Dr. David DeLong, a research fellow at the MIT AgeLab, author, speaker, and consultant to a blue-chip roster of organizations that include Microsoft, Dow, Pepsico, MetLife, and AARP. His book *Lost Knowledge: Confronting the Threat of an Aging Workforce* details the damage caused by the loss of critical organizational knowledge and intellectual capital when older workers retire. The book is packed with case histories and examines how such organizations as NASA, Siemens, the Tennessee Valley Authority, Sandia National Laboratories, Shell Chemical, and the World Bank have dealt with the issue of knowledge retention.

It may not be happening fast enough for BoomerPreneurs such as Morris. "Much is being written but little is being done to repair the damage to a corporation when losing the valuable experience of an older employee," he told me. He does see some signs of this changing and has enjoyed a positive reaction to his latest project – an online clearinghouse that would enable boomers to leverage their networks to deliver qualified leads to companies looking to sell products to commercial clients. The boomers would also be able to offer their own services, or the services of friends and associates, on a part-time or project basis, to companies in the network. This would enable companies to take advantage of the contacts and the skills of boomers on a pay-as-go basis, while enabling boomers to efficiently tap into a network of companies that would value either their skills or, perhaps more importantly, their Rolodexes (or perhaps I should say, their Outlook contacts).

The millennial generation will experience further pressure as companies do start to rethink their attitudes toward older workers – even enabling workers to come out of retirement. But anything that blurs the lines of "traditional retirement" – that causes more attention to be paid to the possibilities of engaging older workers – is bound to create another barrier along the traditional entry-level pathways the millennials are now attempting to traverse. Especially if these new attitudes are not just in grudging response to laws against age discrimination but are deliberate, rational strategies intended to increase productivity and competitiveness.

The opportunity to deploy boomer and senior skills on a temporary basis is particularly attractive to employers. These skills can go beyond the basics of organizational skills, work ethic, and a willingness to follow systems: They can be tailored more precisely to specific situations. The *New York Times* carried a story in April 2009 by Michael Winerip, in which he described how a financial services company deployed a special team of older temporary workers to field calls from angry investors who were suddenly discovering the serious erosion of their retirement funds. "The company wanted its temporary workers to have the patience, maturity and experience to handle the onslaught of calls from older investors panicked about retirement savings," Winerip reports. He cites the case of a team member who had to console an elderly woman who had lost so much of her retirement savings money that she had to go back to work, even though she was now in her late 70s. "I stayed on the phone with her nearly half an hour," the team member reported. "I had nothing in particular to talk to her about, but she was in a quandary, she needed comfort." Winerip adds:

> *That kind of service is why Carol Ringer, a senior human resources manager for the financial company, which agreed to discuss its strategy on the condition that it not be named, intends to bring back the boomer team at the start of each quarter. And that's also why she is paying them 20 percent more than typical temp employees, who often have 20 to 30 years less experience.*

The older temps were recruited from the Boomer Group, a Denver employment agency started by Stephanie Klein in 2004. "Most temp service companies are run by young people and are for young people," Klein told the reporter. But older workers are more reliable. She said she normally placed 10 to 20 percent more younger temps than a job calls for because there are always a number of no-shows. But with boomers, "if a company asks for five, I don't have to send seven."

Boomers in the Crosshairs

I am not saying there is a one-size-fits-all generational response to the jobs crisis from the boomers and seniors, and a totally different one from the millennials. Nevertheless I believe it is fair to argue that boomers and seniors have the skills, the resources, and the attitude that makes them relatively more effective in the job market than the millennials. Even if they don't all succeed in either hanging on to their job or finding a new one, their collective influence represents just one more (unexpected) hurdle for the millennials to surmount.

One other thing is true. We're seeing a *ton* of Age Rage on this subject – angry millennials blaming boomers and seniors (but particularly boomers) for having messed things up for them, and grouchy (or outright unsympathetic) boomers and seniors pushing back.

I'm going to give only a few examples, but trust me when I tell you that you could spend days and days working your way through angry websites and hate-filled blog posts. I won't say all millennials share the same viewpoint – there are, as I will show, some who are willing to shoulder some of the responsibility – but the overwhelming impression is one of resentment. Resentment fueled by surprise ("How can this be happening to us?") and finger-pointing ("It's all the fault of the boomers").

A good example to start with is an exchange on AnswersYahoo.com, in which someone seriously posed the question: "Why won't the Baby Boomers step aside?" Here is the question in full (unedited):

> *In 2011 it is extremely hard for a college graduate to find a job. Why won't the baby boomer generation just retire so younger people can have a chance? I figure they've enjoyed years of income and if responsible have saved money to retire on. I'm a college graduate with a BS in Health Science and cannot find a job. I've been working delivering pizza's for the last year. I can barely pay for*

food. I live in utter poverty and may become homeless if this keeps up. Baby boomers need to accept that they've had a good run and pass on the torch to the younger generation. I don't enjoy shopping at ALDI for groceries and living in an area where my apartment gets broken into twice a year. Why is it that someone in babyboomer generation was able to get a job with only a high school diploma that would require a masters today?

The question provokes a variety of answers that offer variations on the theme of boomer greed and selfishness. One or two will give you the flavor. In all cases, I have kept the punctuation and errors in spelling and grammar, etc., as in the original.

Seriously they are just being plain greedy. its getting into a bass ackwards cycle now because they won't retire and grads are forced to move back in with their parents. who cares if you don't have a million dollars to retire on? life will work itself out you don't need to be 60 and still working. why don't the baby boomers take the imaginary entry positions if they want to continue to work and let the grad students have a career instead of a part time job? ... the baby boomers had their time, and it is time for the next generation.

The boomers push back vigorously, explaining why they won't – and in fact, shouldn't – "step aside."

Because many of us are too busy supporting our college graduate kids who refuse to shop at Walmart or live in shaky neighborhoods. And some of us are simultaneously taking care of our parents as well – you know, your Grandma and Grandpa? Or maybe you want us to retire so you can take care of ALL of us as well as yourself on your fresh-out-of-college income? ... although it's true I got my first job with only a high school diploma, guess what? I wouldn't be working now if that's all I had.

> *I went on and got a degree just like you did. The only difference may be that I put in my time shopping at thrift stores and living in sketchy neighborhoods for years while I worked to get where I am today. And now that I'm here, I'll stay here as long as I need to.*
>
> *Because we spent all our retirement money educating our kids who won't even bother to call ...*
>
> *We made a way that suited our times and so should you. And BTW, you are NOT getting my job. Crybaby.*

On a much larger and more sophisticated scale, *The Atlantic* magazine asked its millennial readers to share their experiences of looking for work. The results were rolled into a collection the magazine described as *Profiles of the Jobless: The 'Mad as Hell' Millennial Generation*. A few excerpts will suffice.

> *The baby boomers say from the comfort of lower unemployment and a stable mortgage there's no escaping the pain. They are more concerned with keeping inflation low then [sic] the unemployment of their children. They are more interested in protecting their 401K and Social Security benefits than investing in tomorrow. They spent our future and now need us to pay the costs.*
>
> *Some say that we should not expect things to be handed to us, and that we should just stop whining. That may be the case for some, but what about those of us who never expected anything? There are thousands of us who worked hard and did everything we were supposed to do. We were told, "If you push yourself and work harder than everyone else, you will succeed." We did not create the problems our nation is facing today. We didn't vote for the politicians, we didn't borrow too much money, we didn't buy things we couldn't afford, and we didn't build the hopes and dreams of an entire generation, only to have them come crashing down.*
>
> *Nothing infuriates me more as a Millennial than*

the self-righteousness of the Baby Boomers. Their entire lives have been all take and no give.

Millennials in the Crosshairs

To be fair, not all of the comments are in this vein. The same person who observed that the baby boomers "spent our future and now need us to pay the costs" ended with this ruthless self-assessment:

Most of my anger is reserved for myself. I pursued a "Liberal Arts Degree" in communications rather than a B.S. in engineering or computer science. I spent all four years at a state university rather than the first two at a community college. I worked in the summer instead of getting an internship. I worked harder at my classes than making contacts and networking with professionals. Not everyone is suffering in this economy, and if I were going to college for the first time this fall I'd know how to prepare. But I didn't at the time and now I'm left to face the consequences. I want to blame the universities and "grown-ups" who I feel should have known better. They were the ones, after all, peddling the mantra of "go to college, study hard, get a job." Instead, egotistical like the rest of my me-first, entitlement-ridden generation, I blame myself.

Some of those sentiments – plus a lot of other negative observations – are echoed by boomers invited by *The Atlantic* to give their side of the story. They're not exactly breaking out the handkerchiefs for the millennials. Here's a small sampling:

Shorter version of Millennial rant: "Waah! Those horrible Boomers! I really want to live an entitled life like they had, and I deserve, but they messed everything up. Instead, I actually have to start at the bottom like every other generation. How unfair!"

> There are 79 million boomers. We were all druggies in
> bell bottoms and mini skirts who went all yuppie on y'all.
> Viet Nam was our fault. The Federal Reserve is our fault.
> The entitlement society is our fault. And you graduated
> and can't get a job. That's our fault, too. But that is what
> parents do. Absorb the shocks from their grown up babies
> and keep on loving them while they figure out the world
> does not rotate around their ass.
>
> Too many people believe they will be protected,
> comforted, and provided for by the state that made them
> promises. That has bred a kind of extended adolescence,
> lasting in some cases for a lifetime. Fortunately, a lot of
> people are belatedly realizing this.
>
> So, you're all sentenced to that frozen gulag of a
> re-education camp, otherwise known as real life.

The boomers and seniors have their story, and their point of view, but my bet is that while it *will* prevail in the marketplace, it won't prevail in the world of opinions and ideas. The number of boomer academics, pundits, journalists, and opinion makers who feel guilty about their generation's deficiencies, and are happy to validate the anger of the millennials, is not small. The meme of boomer selfishness and greed will likely overcome the meme of millennial immaturity and dysfunction, leaving the millennials as the aggrieved victims and the boomers as the thoughtless oppressors.

The Case Against the Boomers

After all, the case against the boomers – in social or moral terms – is not inconsequential. Here is Walter Russell Mead again, on his blog ViaMedia. He tells boomers that the backlash against them has begun

> at the level of public policy and moral leadership,
> as a generation we have largely failed. The Boomer
> Progressive Establishment in particular has been a

huge disappointment to itself and to the country. The political class slumbered as the entitlement and pension crisis grew to ominous dimensions. Boomer financial leadership was selfish and shortsighted, by and large. Boomer CEOs accelerated the trend toward unlimited greed among corporate elites, and Boomer members of corporate boards sit by and let it happen. Boomer academics created a profoundly dysfunctional system that systemically shovels resources upward from students and adjuncts to overpaid administrators and professors who by and large have not, to say the least, done an outstanding job of transmitting the cultural heritage of the past to future generations.

Not surprisingly, he says, there was bound to be a reaction. "Sooner or later, the kids were going to note what a mess we have many of so many things …" But there is hope for redemption. "There is still time to do better. We can, for example, step up to the plate and sacrifice a few benefits, putting the well being of future generations ahead of our own." Mead calls for the boomers to save money, rebuild community and religious institutions, and "gracefully step back to give new generations more of a chance." Not that this will be enough to redeem the boomer image: "It is too late for us to be remembered as a generation of wise statesmen, great leaders, selfless role models, responsible business people, faithful spouses, sacrificial parents, and builders and renewers of great institutions."

One could argue, after first shaking one's head and wondering if *any* sins have been omitted, that the moral argument Mead offers – what the boomers *ought* to do – is eloquent and compelling. Many boomers, however, would not sign up for Mead's guilt or his sweeping to-do list.

A survey of US baby boomers, conducted in 2011 by the investment firm U.S. Trust, showed that less than half of the *wealthiest* boomers – i.e., the ones most able to do so

– thought it was important to leave money to their children. In an article on this research on *Time*'s Moneyland website, Brad Tuttle comments: "After decades of personal and professional sacrifices for the sake of their children, and after paying for their kids' educations and perhaps helping them with down payments on first homes, boomers have reached the point that enough is enough."

He goes on to note: "Boomer parents haven't stopped worrying about their kids. Instead, what aging boomers seem to be saying, through the survey and their actions, is that they don't have much confidence in their children's financial sense, and throwing more money at them isn't going to help. So why not just use the money to enjoy yourself and take that round-the-world cruise?"

They certainly did seem to be saying that in the survey. Some 20% of the boomers were afraid their kids would squander any inheritance, while 25% thought an inheritance would make the children lazier. Just over half (52%) didn't even tell the kids how much they were worth.

As an expression of boomer attitudes toward millennials, these research findings appear to provide more ammunition in support of the idea of bad feeling between the generations, possibly even top-down Age Rage. It's easy to jump to the conclusion that this proves that the greedy boomers are looking out for themselves first, last, and always – a conclusion that prompts imagery of a war against the young.

But take a closer look. Reread Tuttle's first observation, to the effect that boomers have arrived at "enough is enough" only after decades of kids-first sacrifice. Keep in mind that half of the boomers don't share this attitude. And, as we will see later, even among those who do, there is a difference between saying "enough is enough" and declining to show up with needed support one more time.

The boomers, as they have done all of their lives, are quite capable of reconciling conflicting needs, wants, and even values – in this case, aggressiveness in the job market and the political fight for health-care and pension entitlements (which their critics decry as a "me first" attitude), on the one hand, with a readiness to shore up the floundering millennials (who are, after all, the boomers' children and grandchildren), on the other. This book will conclude with a detailed look at this shoring-up process. But before that, let's turn to the second front of the apparent war – the political battleground.

The Political Battle

By its very nature, the job market front, covered in the previous chapter, does not force a zero sum solution. In theory, both armies could win. In fact, soldiers of both of our armies *do* win every single day: Some boomers hold on to their jobs and seniors successfully re-enter the workforce, and some millennials graduate and get hired. Success for one doesn't have to preclude success for the other.

The battleground on the political front, the subject of this and the following chapter, is something else again.

It is true that our vast governments include programs that target both groups – education for the young, pensions and health-care benefits for the old. It is also true that, no matter how bad the economy, funding for either side is not going to drop to zero. But once we've dispensed with that simple and obvious fact, we're left with a struggle that can be more focused and intense than the battle for jobs. Governments all over the world have run out of money and are now running out of their capacity to borrow. Shrinking economies are giving rise to lower tax revenues. The pressure to cut costs cannot be resisted. Painful tradeoffs will have to be made.

We must note, right off the bat, that governments are beset by *many* competing armies, not just older vs. younger. There are battles between unions and corporations. There are battles within the corporate sector, as different industries and interest groups jockey for favored positions and the continued receipt of government largesse – subsidies, tax credits, protective tariffs. There are also battles within levels of government – federal, provincial or state, local. Each is in financial trouble, each is pushing for a bigger piece of the shrinking tax-revenue pie, battling each other in the court of public opinion, and, with increased frequency, in the courts of law.

There are over 17,000 registered lobby groups in the USA, and almost 3,000 registered lobby groups in Canada. That's at the national level in both countries. Add to that state or provincial groups, local groups, levels of government lobbying each other, think tanks, specialty media, ad hoc social media groups that can be created in minutes, and it adds up to a non-stop avalanche of pressure on all levels of government. So our two armies are far from being the only combatants.

But that makes it only more important for them to be able to fight effectively. As we will see, it's an unequal struggle.

We should note, too, that not all members of the competing generations are after the same things. Both armies contain left-wing as well as right-wing members. Both armies contain people who are doing relatively well and people who are struggling. Both armies contain people for whom it is vital that their problems be fixed in the very short term and people whose situations are less urgent. Both contain people who are passionate and willing to work hard for the cause and those who may believe in the cause but essentially are along for the ride.

All that said, I think it is relatively easy to identify certain broad trends in terms of what the competing armies are after, and how effectively they are battling.

The Two Forces: Key Issues

The key issues for the boomers and seniors involve pensions and health-care benefits. They don't want to lose their existing entitlements. They are very worried, from both practical and ideological standpoints, about government spending and government debt levels, but they also want to make sure that any necessary cutbacks don't encroach on their entitlements or their access to needed services.

The key issues for the millennials involve education – a reduction in tuition fees, more grants or loans, and relief from the huge debts they have already incurred.

There is also a general grumbling, on the part of millennials, about the level of government debt that the boomers are leaving behind – debt that the millennials recognize will have to be discharged from their future earnings. Underfunded entitlement programs will have to be brought into line, and even if there are cutbacks in future benefits, even if there is a gradual phasing-in of higher ages at which eligibility will kick in, the millennials can foresee years (maybe a lifetime) of higher taxes to pay for the fiscal sins of the boomers.

So we have some very natural, and understandable, sets of competing interests at play here.

- There is widespread fear that health-care costs will rise to unaffordable levels as the population continues to age

- There is spirited debate about the huge levels of unfunded pension liabilities (this is particularly true in the USA), differences in pension entitlements of government workers vs. private sector workers, and the impossibility of sustaining current entitlement levels going forward

- There are the beginnings of debate (more advanced in the USA but starting to happen now in Canada as well) about the costs of education and the efficacy of the system, particularly in relation to its ability to train students for the real-world job market

We need not delve too deeply into the specifics of each issue. The topics are complex, and the arguments pro and con can change radically depending on whether the view adopted is short-, medium- or long-term. For our purposes, it's enough to note that the issues will *not* be able to be addressed by simply spreading more money around, for the good reason that there isn't enough money available. More than ever, increased spending in one area must mean decreased spending in another.

But it's worse than just dollar-for-dollar swapping between existing spending levels. Governments are also under tremendous pressure to cut *the total level* of spending. In the past, spending cuts could be disguised as decreases in the rate of increase. Going forward, that seems less likely, if only because the financial markets are beginning to push back. Because of the tremendous complexity of government today, however, it will likely be too difficult to cut spending with a simple across-the-board percentage decrease. There are statutory issues, intergovernmental jurisdiction and funding issues, uneven social and political costs – not to mention the iron law of politics: Whatever you do, your first priority is to get re-elected. Some programs will be cut, others will survive; some cuts will be deep, others less so; some savings will be realized now, others will be realized (keep your fingers crossed) in the future.

All this puts a premium on effective lobbying. How loudly and effectively can you state your case? How forcefully can you influence the politicians?

That is the issue for us in this chapter. Our focus is not on the question of whether the causes of the boomers/seniors or the causes of the millennials are right or wrong, or whether the proposed solutions are good or bad. It is on the fight itself and who's likely to prevail and why.

The Size of the Armies

Let's start with comparing the size of the two armies. Size matters, of course, because ultimately we're talking about votes.

In both Canada and the USA, the millennials are completely outgunned.

Much has been made about the youth vote, but the truth is, it isn't nearly as important as the boomer and senior vote. I'm not saying politicians shouldn't go after it – if you're a politician, you'd like *any* voter to vote for you. But in the aggregate, there aren't enough young voters to carry the day, and this is all the more so if the older voters are energized.

Here, based on data from Elections Canada and the US Census Bureau, is the percentage of *votes actually cast*, by each age group, in the 2008 elections in the USA and Canada.

Percentage of Votes Cast by Age Group

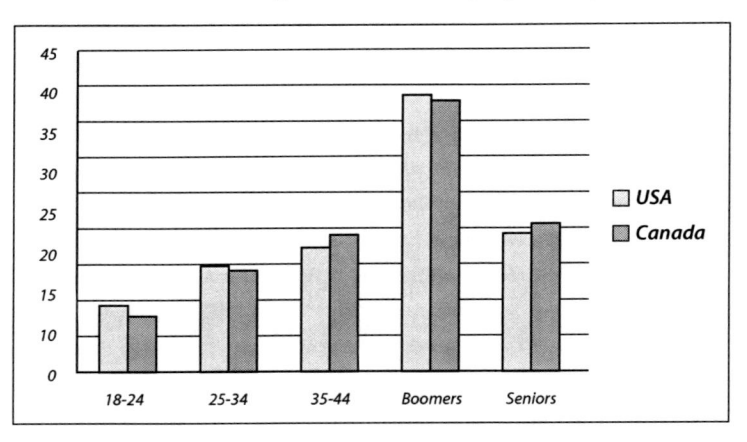

Now let's combine the 18 to 24 and 25 to 34 age groups and call it the millennials (it actually inflates the millennial total slightly, because technically the bloc of those ages 31 to 34 belong to Generation X). Let's also combine the boomers and seniors. Following is how the two voting groups compare.

Percentage of Votes Cast by Combined Age Groups

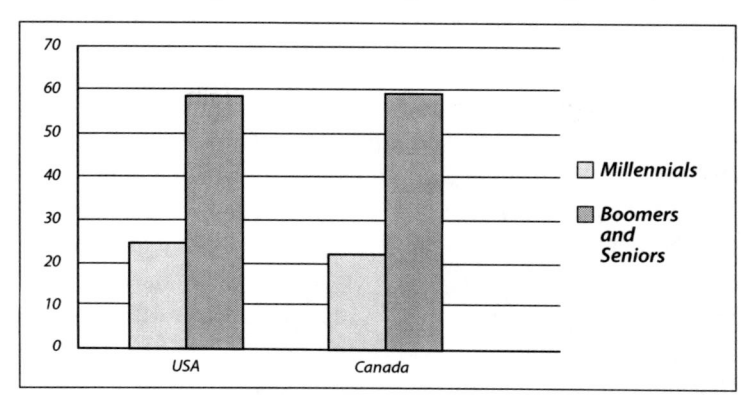

[Bar chart showing USA and Canada voting percentages with Millennials and Boomers and Seniors categories]

The actual numbers are:

- USA: millennials, 24.4%; boomers and seniors, 58.2%
- Canada: millennials, 22.1%; boomers and seniors, 58.8%

Remember, these are percentages of votes actually cast. If we subtract out the Gen Xers who are included in the group ages 25 to 34, we're looking at almost a 3 to 1 ratio of votes cast, in favor of the boomers and seniors.

The results should not be surprising. The boomers and seniors are a much larger population, and their margin is further compounded because their turnout rate is much higher than that of the millennials. In both Canada and the USA, voter turnout rates climb steadily as the voter segment gets older, ranging from under 50% for those 18 to 24 years old to nudging about 70% for the oldest seniors.

But do they all vote the same way? Are they motivated only by generational concerns? Why not by ideology? And who's to say all the members of a generation have identical concerns anyway? Why, for example, shouldn't there be a significant number of sympathetic boomers and seniors who might identify with the needs of the millennials rather than those of their own age group? Certainly I have presented more than a few strident anti-boomer screeds written by ... boomers. Wouldn't such people be more likely to be marching off to war on the side of the millennials?

These are all fair questions, and I am posing them so you don't have to. I don't want them festering in the back of your mind as you read what follows. I don't want you wondering if I'm avoiding them to favor my line of argument. So let's address the issue right up front.

Numerous studies suggest that people do get more conservative as they get older. While this does not necessarily translate into bloc voting for one party or another, the broad trend is that, with age, people are more liable to favor less radical solutions to public policy issues and be more focused on dollars and cents.

This makes sense intuitively. By the time you're in your 50s and 60s, you've had decades of eyewitness experience concerning what works and what doesn't and how noble rhetoric often turns into grubby compromise. You no longer have the same stars in your eyes as you did when you were much younger. This doesn't necessarily make you a reactionary, and it doesn't necessarily mean you're a knee-jerk big-C Conservative voter in Canada or a Republican voter in the USA. But it does present a more fertile ground for parties of the center-right or right.

In the USA, for example, Gallup tracking polls show that the percentage of voters who self-identify as small-c conservative is double the percentage of those who self-identify as small-l liberal.

At the other end of the spectrum, polls suggest that the millennials are more likely to be liberal and to favor statist solutions to public policy problems. In fact, a 2008 study, *The Millennial Pendulum*, published by the New America Foundation <www.newamerica.net>, says the millennials are more liberal not only than the older generations but also than the boomers themselves were at the same age.

The political attitudes and policy preferences of Millennials reinforce their liberal self-concept. They are far less likely than their elders and than the other generations when they were young to feel that the government wastes a lot of money. They had more progressive attitudes to the general population on federal aid to schools and were just as likely as the elder respondents to say that the government should provide universal health insurance.

The big factor – even before we discuss political organization and lobbying and compare the effectiveness of the two armies – is voter turnout. If the older voters turn out in greater proportion (multiplied by their going-in advantage in population), the results can be more skewed to the conservative agenda – big-C or small-c. And this would favor the agenda of the boomers and seniors even if they weren't highly organized and aggressive (which, as we will see, they certainly are). From the millennials' point of view, the fact that they are outnumbered and face a state of opinion that is broadly more conservative than theirs puts a premium on their being highly organized and effective.

The voter turnout issue, as it plays out in Canada, is well described in a column by Tim Harper in the *Toronto Star* in June 2011, "Have We Become a Conservative Country?" Harper says Canada "is not necessarily a conservative country, but the people who vote in this country are Conservatives." He cites the "startling conclusion" that Frank Graves of EKOS Research came to when he analyzed voting patterns from the May 2 general election:

If voters under 45 had voted in the same numbers as those over 45, Graves said, the Conservatives under Stephen Harper would not only have been denied a majority government, they could be sitting in opposition to a centre-left coalition led by Jack Layton.

Let's pause to note that "could be sitting in opposition" covers a lot of ground. If the point is that Harper would not have had a majority, that's perfectly sound. If the point is that the centrist Liberal Party and the left-wing New Democratic Party (then under the brilliant leadership of Jack Layton, since deceased) could have/would have formed, and ruled as, a coalition government – even though neither party had more seats than the Conservatives – this is somewhat more speculative. So let's go back to the main line of argument, which is much more solid.

- The median age in this country is now 42
    It was 26 in our Centennial year of 1967
    It is one of the oldest median ages in the world
    (Graves says the median age in the Islamic world is 17)
- Some 15% of the population is over 65, but this is the demographic that votes, overwhelming for the Conservatives, with a voter turnout rate in the 70-80% range, Graves found
- In the 18 to 30 age group, Conservative support struggles to hit 20%. But only about 35% of them vote, Graves says

I don't want to push the argument beyond where it can go. All I'm saying is that the ground is more favorable for the boomers and seniors even before the battle is joined. They outnumber the millennials, their point of view is shared by more people than that of the millennials, and they turn out to vote in much greater numbers than the millennials.

Before the first shots are fired, then, it isn't exactly an even contest.

Let's see what happens once they *are* fired.

The Boomer Army: Organization

The boomers and seniors have always been well organized and have long-standing and highly efficient organizations that lobby for their interests.

In the USA, there is AARP, which became a part of American culture by its ability to identify, and send a birthday card to, every American on the occasion of their 50th birthday. The organization boasts a membership in the range of 40 million. It is recognized as one of the most influential lobby groups in the USA. Its twin 10-storey headquarters in downtown Washington, D.C., screams power and proximity to power.

AARP offers information, services, and discounts to its members. Most of the concrete benefits that it offers cluster in the area of health insurance plans: The lack of decent health insurance for retired teachers was the primary driver in the creation of AARP in the first place, more than 50 years ago. Services include how-to information as well as programs such as the job fairs we looked at in the previous chapter. AARP's magazine has the largest circulation of any magazine in the USA; the organization also maintains a large website, supplemented by e-newsletters and targeted e-blasts on specific topics.

AARP has had some difficulties in recent years. It lost tens of thousands of members because of its perceived over-enthusiasm for President Obama's health-care reforms. It has also been in trouble with regulatory agencies over real or perceived conflicts of interest in the marketing of its health insurance products. Competitors – such as the American Seniors Association – have come into being, appealing to those with a more conservative point of view. While no one rival organization comes close to AARP's size or influence, collectively they have several million dues-paying members.

With a multi-million-dollar marketing communications budget and increasingly sophisticated digital and social media tools, AARP is able to quickly mobilize its members and exert strong pressure on elected representatives.

In Canada, there is CARP (like AARP, its name was originally spelled out – Canadian Association of Retired Persons – but now only the initials are used). CARP has become very influential on the Canadian political scene and is now recognized by all the news media as the established go-to source for comments and ideas on all issues related to boomers and seniors.

In 2009, Canadian media innovator Moses Znaimer became President of CARP. He had acquired the organization's magazine and amalgamated it and other media assets, including two radio stations and a portfolio of websites, into a public company, ZoomerMedia Limited. ZoomerMedia also acquired the exclusive rights to provide membership and marketing services to CARP. (Full disclosure: At the time of writing I am employed by ZoomerMedia and am also a member of the Board of Directors of CARP.)

ZoomerMedia has since expanded through acquisition and development and now also includes Vision TV, Canada's only multi-faith specialty television service; ONE: The Body, Mind, Spirit and Love Channel, which offers programs on exercise, meditation, yoga, and natural health; Joytv 10 in Vancouver and Joytv 22 in Winnipeg; a thriving shows division that includes the Zoomer Show, the largest consumer show devoted exclusively to this age group (the 2012 schedule includes shows in Toronto, Ottawa, Calgary and Vancouver); and Idea City, an annual conference also known as "Canada's premier meeting of the minds."

Znaimer changed the name of the magazine to *ZOOMER* magazine, and rebranded CARP under the mantra "A New Vision of Aging for Canada." With his famous flair for against-the-tide creativity, he decided not to flee from the acronym, which had some obvious negatives and which the previous regime had contemplated abandoning. Rather, he embraced the fish and turned it into a cheeky, and memorable, emblem.

Znaimer also brought in Susan Eng to be Vice President of Advocacy. A former tax lawyer, community activist, and media commentator, she had served as Chair of the Metropolitan Toronto Police Services Board from 1991 to 1995 and was also co-chair of the Ontario Coalition of Chinese Head Tax Payers and Families, campaigning successfully for a Parliamentary apology and redress for the *Head Tax and Exclusion Act*. So she had a deep understanding of how to advocate and how to influence the political process.

Under the direction of Znaimer and Eng, CARP advocacy quickly became more focused, sophisticated, and effective. The organization developed a reputation for excellent policy research; Eng testifies frequently before committees of the federal Parliament and many provincial legislatures. This, combined with the powerful media network that CARP is associated with, has increased CARP's profile dramatically.

For example, CARP has begun staging debates in association with local, provincial, and national elections – debates that political parties, knowing the high level of PR that CARP can generate and the fact that the debates are telecast and webcast through Zoomer's own channels, dare not miss.

CARP has also succeeded in leveraging the results of online polling of its members. It is not uncommon for CARP polls to generate over 5,000 responses – within days – and Susan Eng and her team are quick to communicate the polling results to politicians and policy makers (as well as to publicize them in ZoomerMedia channels and the broader media). CARP's ability to jump on an issue, poll the membership, and communicate the results in order to reinforce its advocacy positions – all of this backed up by aggressive media coverage in the ZoomerMedia channels to which CARP has immediate access – has meant politicians cannot ignore the demands of CARP's constituency.

As a result of all these efforts, CARP has already had some major successes.

For example, CARP demanded higher payments to seniors receiving the federal Guaranteed Income Supplement. Recipients are, by definition, living in poverty, so every additional dollar is critically important. CARP conducted polls of its members and let the politicians know that more than 60% of them were ready to switch parties over the issue of helping the most vulnerable.

The politicians got the message.

During the federal election campaign (spring 2011), all of the major parties promised to increase the GIS. The Conservatives offered $300 million, which would cover 680,000 of the poorest seniors. The Liberals pledged $700 million, while the New Democratic Party promised whatever it would take to raise every senior out of poverty immediately.

CARP commented, in the 2011 annual report of its advocacy efforts:

> *The parties were outbidding one another for the seniors' vote. It was the right thing to do but they also got CARP's message that older Canadians vote at higher rates, at every level, than any other group of Canadians. So when CARP called for a longer-term view and a comprehensive strategy to ensure that no Canadian senior lives in poverty, the political parties listened. When the dust settled on the election, we got a $300 million increase to the GIS and by now, hundreds of thousands of seniors across the country will have received bigger GIS cheques. There is still some distance to go to get to "whatever it takes" to lift every senior out of poverty, but one thing is certain: addressing financial security among older Canadians is now a political imperative.*

Just how true this is was demonstrated in the furor over possible changes to the Old Age Security program, another component of the federal pension system that targets the neediest seniors. This is a classic case of how quickly and effectively CARP can mobilize its base.

The trouble started with a speech by Canadian Prime Minister Stephen Harper to the World Economic Forum in Davos, Switzerland, on January 26, 2012. "Western nations," he declared, "face a choice of whether to create the conditions for growth and prosperity, or to risk long-term economic decline. In every decision, or failure to decide, we are choosing our future right now."

Harper touched on a range of topics – oil and gas exploration, immigration, free trade – but the one that set off the firestorm was the aging population. "We've already taken steps to limit the growth of our health-care spending," he said, referring to the new funding formula that will gradually reduce federal health-care subsidies to the provinces. "We must do the same for our retirement income system."

Harper did not offer any specifics, but post-speech speculation immediately centered on the Old Age Security (OAS) program. Unlike the Canada Pension Plan, which is financed by contributions and (in contrast to the Social Security program in the USA) is well funded and sustainable, the OAS program is funded out of government revenues. It cost the government $36.5 billion in 2010, and some actuarial reports estimate that, absent changes, the cost could approach $50 billion by 2015 and top $100 billion by 2030. Eligibility kicks in at age 65, although benefits are clawed back based on other income, effectively limiting the program to the neediest seniors.

There are a number of ways to deal with this. The program could continue as now constructed with the costs handled through savings in other areas of government spending. (The resource-allocation line of argument with which we're already familiar.) There could be changes in the clawback formula. Or the age of eligibility could be raised so that the program doesn't kick in until, say, age 67.

It was this last point on which all the attention quickly focused.

Although Harper gave no specifics in his speech, critics immediately opened fire, accusing the government of planning to raise the age of eligibility in the very short term. Opposition Leader Bob Rae, of the Liberal Party, charged that "the Prime Minister has broken his word to Canadians on a subject that is of great concern to them, and that is their security in old age. And it is unbelievable to me that the Prime Minister would be allowed to get away with this."

Rae was no doubt thinking about previous governments that had contemplated tinkering with the OAS and had not been "allowed to get away with this." Both the Conservatives, under Prime Minister Brian Mulroney, and Rae's Liberal Party, under Prime Minister Jean Chretien, had made opening moves on OAS reform but had to back down in the face of public anger.

The Conservatives quickly tried a walk-back on Harper's speech. Both Harper and Finance Minister Jim Flaherty stated that nobody currently receiving OAS benefits, or near the age of retirement, would be affected by any changes – implying that the changes would be phased in gradually. But they still gave no specifics.

Not good enough for CARP and Susan Eng.

Within a few days of Harper's speech, Eng was all over the media – not just the ZoomerMedia channels, but all the major TV networks and newspapers in Canada – attacking the idea of increasing the age of OAS eligibility and, tellingly, reminding the government of the importance of the senior vote. CARP quickly created a HANDS OFF OAS page on its website, and produced a poll showing that a significant number of members would be willing to switch their political allegiance over the issue: 60% of over 3,000 respondents to the poll said they strongly opposed any such action, and support for the Conservatives dropped from 44% prior to Harper's speech to 35% after. Not a small reaction, to put it mildly.

Not everyone is happy about CARP's effectiveness. In a perfect illustration of the Age Rage phenomenon, *Globe and Mail* columnist Margaret Wente went after CARP in her February 2, 2012, column "Where Have We Seen This Before? – The War Against the Young."

Wente described CARP as "the aptly named association for retired people," noting that "CARP is always carping about something." She predicted a long-term adjustment in OAS, stating that CARP's "histrionics ignore the fact that any changes to OAS wouldn't come for years and wouldn't affect a single person who's currently a senior, or anything close to it." Then she got to the crux of the issue, as she sees it.

> *Now, our biggest social problem is not how to redistribute more money to the needy old. It's how to protect everyone else from the tsunami of geezers that's about to crash on our shores and suck the wealth of future generations out to sea. The war against seniors' pension reforms is a war against the young.*

Insisting she's not against seniors, Wente says "we need to think about how we allocate our money. Are we really sure we want to transfer so much wealth from struggling young families to well-off geezers? ... How many schools won't get built because we're buying Lipitor for people who can already afford to pay for it?"

The solution?

"I think anyone with a social conscience and a CARP membership should tear it up."

The column, when posted to the Globe and Mail website, produced an astonishing 983 comments in just a few days. Pro and con, feelings ran high.

CARP responded on its own website, offering a rebuttal to the points raised in Wente's column and then concluding:

> *And a final thank you to Ms Wente, for reminding readers that CARP is a membership organization and depends on their support to make our voice heard when governments attack our collective sense of well-being. Our phones have been ringing off the hook and the online sign-up page is crashing. But keep trying.*

As of early March, the Harper government still had not offered any specifics on how it planned to change OAS. As this book went to press, details were expected to be forthcoming in the federal budget, scheduled for the end of March. It's significant, however, that Harper struck a fairly conciliatory tone in his comments to the editorial board of the *National Post*, published on February 4.

Speaking of the financial crisis in Europe, a big component of which is unfunded pension expectations, he noted that some governments "are being forced to cut benefits to people when they really need them." This is not the case in Canada, he asserted. "I don't think we need to be in that position. I think we can examine these issues now and deal with problems before they are upon us."

He then went on to say that "we are not looking at changes that are going to affect people that are currently in retirement or approaching retirement. We've been very clear on that." Then again, later in the interview: "I think we have been very clear in our electoral mandate that we're not going to make any changes to seniors or to pensions in any way that deals with the current deficit."

This last comment seems to imply that Harper's government is not expecting to find immediate savings in OAS – savings that could impact its current deficit issues – and that any changes would be longer-term. If so, this would defuse much of the criticism, since everyone, CARP included, is open to longer-term adjustments that could be very gradual, with runways that will give people plenty of time to adjust their plans.

But to the extent that the Harper government does act in the shorter term, as Susan Eng promised on national TV, "They will have a political fight on their hands."

One final important point should be noted, and it plays into the final chapter, where we will look at how the boomers and seniors are solving the war of the generations. You could argue that, if they were motivated only by selfishness, CARP and its members wouldn't bother with the OAS at all. Why is CARP so engaged when most of its members would not be directly affected and if the government (as seems likely at the time of writing, in early March) will not tamper with the benefits of current recipients? Because CARP and a significant portion of its membership care about the less fortunate, who could be in financial trouble if the government increases the age at which OAS eligibility kicks in, even if that increase lies several years ahead. CARP's members, then, are demonstrably *not* motivated by their immediate self-interest alone. They are looking ahead to understand what it will mean to be a senior and be in poverty. They are determined to be engaged, and influential, in policy discussions concerning this topic.

This point is important in the context of the thesis of moving beyond Age Rage, not so much because of the ins and outs of pension reform itself but because of what it says about the attitudes and motivations of the older generations. As vigorously as they fight for their immediate needs, wants, and interests, they are also able to look beyond themselves.

The Millennial Army: Organization

The examples of CARP in Canada and AARP in the USA demonstrate the kind of organizational and media clout that can be brought to bear on behalf of the issues that affect boomers and seniors. Is there equivalent firepower on the millennial side?

The Canadian Federation of Students claims 500,000 members and lobbies on behalf of university students. Membership is through individual campus associations. Advocacy efforts focus on the expected topics – university funding, tuition fees, student loans. The federation employs full-time researchers and makes frequent presentations to all levels of government. Interestingly, the federation acknowledges on the home page of its website its need to be seen to have large numbers.

> *No individual students' union, no matter how big or active, has the resources or the political clout to effectively influence the post-secondary education policies of the*

provincial and federal governments on its own. At best, an individual students' union could have an impact on only a few federal electoral ridings. Governments ignore groups that pose no political threat to them. It is also much more cost effective for a large number of students' unions to pool their resources and work in partnership than for each to undertake this work on its own. The Federation serves this purpose, giving campus students' unions across the country a united voice and powerful influence.

The federation makes university students, as a bloc, more powerful than they would be through the efforts of individual campus associations. But as this quote acknowledges, the numbers are the numbers. The federation claims 500,000 members, but students do not actually join the federation directly; they are members by virtue of their membership in individual campus associations. So there is a natural fall-off in activity by students, or even in their awareness of the federation's existence and activities.

The federation's total constituency of university and college students is just under one million, compared with CARP's almost 15 million Zoomers. Furthermore, CARP's constituency has an election turnout rate of over 50% and as high as 70%; collectively, the CARP constituency accounts for 6 out of every 10 votes in federal elections. The federation, meanwhile, represents a group with an election turnout rate of only about 35%.

None of this is to disparage the effective work of the federation, which has kept the pressure on Canadian politicians – with some success – to address student issues.

The students have also been able to rally other interested parties, such as public service unions, and, specifically, teachers' unions. In the run-up to the October 2011 Ontario Provincial election, for example, the Elementary Teachers Federation of Ontario (EFTO) ran a TV ad campaign, REFUSE TO VOTE

AGAINST KIDS. The ads attracted a lot of attention and even some controversy because they started with a teaser campaign that seemed to invite people *to* VOTE AGAINST KIDS.

Coming from elementary school teachers, of course, the campaign was not designed to help millennials specifically, but in arguing for no cuts to public education, it staked out the same policy territory. I also found the VOTE AGAINST metaphor interesting, of course, because it seemed to reinforce the attitudinal aspect of intergenerational conflict – to cut public education funding would be to "vote against the kids."

The campaign certainly didn't hurt, and the millennials benefited. The ruling Liberals promised to cut university tuitions by 30% and followed up by introducing a $430-million tuition-rebate program. The program, however, did not give students everything they wanted. It was telling that some of them reacted in the entitlement generation manner.

On February 1, 2012, the *Toronto Star* reported on a rally at Queen's Park, the Ontario provincial capital, to protest the tuition-rebate program. Under the program, students already on a government student loan would automatically qualify for new rebate of $1,600 a year (university students) or $730 a year (community college students).

Wait a minute – protesting *against* these tuition rebates? Yes, because the rebate program did not include mature students, part-time students, or those whose family income was above $160,000.

So the Ontario branch of the Canadian Federation of Students organized a demonstration. But in a surreal touch, the timing coincided with the arrival of the first batch of rebate checks into the bank accounts of recipients. Some demonstrators simultaneously waved protest signs while checking their bank balances on their smart phones.

So we have – in the same week – Susan Eng and CARP and the Canadian Federation of Students at work for their respective constituencies. Quite a study in contrasts.

THE POLITICAL BATTLE

In the USA, the oldest student group is the United States Students Association, formed in 1978 from a merger of the National Student Association and the National Student Lobby. It claims to represent four million students but has only a small fraction of that number as direct members. What's more, the association has been plagued by political controversy. Some individual universities have withdrawn their support due to its politically correct policies, such as requiring that 30% of the board identify as openly "queer," that 50% be "people of color," and that 50% be women.

While the association takes credit, on its website, for achieving a number of policy wins on behalf of students – increases in government funding, better treatment of student loans – there is a long way to go.

> *Each year, students have to fight tooth-and-nail on both the state and federal level to make government invested in fully funding and supporting higher education. It's politically popular for elected officials to advocate for college students and higher education funding. However, most politicians are silent when it comes to education budgets getting slashed. Therefore, it's up to us, the students, to ask our elected officials "where's the funding?!" At a time when the road to socio-economic justice for our communities, personal fulfillment, and a thriving civic society is increasingly tied to higher education, where's the funding to ensure that this path is clear of all unnecessary barriers?*

The association proposes a number of detailed solutions, all part of a "Where's the Funding" campaign that "will connect state and federal budget cuts to the larger student movement, so that we raise a strong national voice on behalf of higher education. Our ultimate goal is to make higher education a right."

A worthy goal, possibly, but inherently undeliverable, because, unlike abstract rights such as freedom of speech, higher education is of necessity tied to funding, and funding is – as we are painfully discovering – finite.

A political issue that enjoys broad support is rare, especially during a contentious budget debate occurring in a painfully jobless economic recovery. Even more rare is when said issue has a base of politically active supporters, giving politicians precious capitol [sic] to do what is both right and popular in a time when common ground seems like foreign soil. Luckily for today's legislators, there is such an issue: higher education.

Sure, except when funding for higher education runs up against funding for pensions and health care.

In prosperous times, when the pie was big enough to more or less take care of everyone, both young and old could, and did, get what they needed. Organizations such as CARP and AARP lobbied over the details of legislation – and these were very important – but didn't face the threat of having their interests sacrificed to higher or more urgent fiscal imperatives such as reducing total government spending to alleviate unsustainable debt. There was really no conflict between their desires and the desires of the students for more educational funding, including more loans and grants.

From the opposite point of view, the student groups did not view their own cause as something that would necessarily eat into the benefits and entitlements of the older generations. There was plenty to go around, and if some alarmists pointed out that "plenty" was arrived at only through borrowing and unfunded future liabilities, nobody was willing to do much about it. Even the draconian spending cuts of the Liberal administration in Canada in the early to mid-1990s were of relatively short duration. What's more, the feds were happy to push the problems of health and education down to the provincial level.

But in today's economy, there is not enough to go around. All interest groups, whether based on age, ideology, or economics (corporations, unions, individual industry sectors), must compete for scarce, if not decreasing, dollars. To voices that have long been in the field – CARP, AARP, student federations – are now added new voices, new organizations that have come to life organically in response to the financial crisis of the times.

It is useful to look at some of these new voices, because we can see a definite contrast between those belonging predominantly to boomers and seniors and those belonging predominantly to the millennials. The nature of this contrast is, in turn, very instructive. It helps us understand intergenerational conflict better – especially the intensity of the war metaphor and the accompanying language and imagery – and it helps us understand how and why the older generations are simultaneously fighting for their own interests and the interests of the other side.

As a case study, I offer the contrast between the Tea Party and the Occupy movements – a vivid illustration of how differently the boomers and millennials operate. Let's take a look.

Generational Effectiveness: A Case Study

*L**ET* us stipulate, at the outset, that any older generation has more knowledge, more experience, and a more effective operational network than any younger generation. That said, a study of the Tea Party and the Occupy movements will reveal certain characteristics of the boomers, and of the millennials, that do not derive simply from their age or length of experience. As the attitudes and expectations of both groups come into play, we see wildly different outcomes in generational effectiveness. I believe the case study casts a stark light on the wider issues examined in this book.

I refer to the Tea Party Express in the USA, and the Occupy movement, which started with Occupy Wall Street in New York and quickly spread to Occupy initiatives around the world.

It is not true, strictly speaking, that the Tea Party movement is for boomers and seniors and the Occupy movement for millennials. Both movements contain members of all age groups, and both movements claim as their driving force a need for specific government action that is not strictly limited to age-related issues. In the case of the Tea Party movement, the goal is dramatic reductions in government spending.

In the case of the Occupy movement, the goal is an end to the inequality that sees 1% of the population making (and keeping) an inordinate amount of money relative to the other 99%.

Nevertheless, a significant majority of Tea Party activists are older, and a significant majority of Occupy activists are younger. What's more, the strategies and tactics of the groups respectively reflect the attitudes, skills, and approaches of the boomers and seniors, on the one hand, and millennials, on the other.

Tea Partiers, Occupiers, and Demographics

First let's nail down the demographics. A spring 2010 survey of Tea Party members conducted by the Winston Group included an age breakdown. You will see that the younger cohorts represent a lower percentage of Tea Party membership than they do in the electorate as a whole, while the reverse is true for the older segments.

Percentage of Age Group Participation in Tea Party vs. Electorate as a Whole		
Ages	Tea Party	Electorate as a Whole
18-34	14%	20%
35-44	14%	17%
45-54	24%	23%
55-64	24%	21%
65+	22%	17%

It's fair to say, then, that if the Tea Party Express is not driven specifically by boomer and senior attitudes, interests, and behaviors, it is at least heavily so informed. Boomers and seniors combined make up 70% of Tea Party membership.

The Occupy movement, on the other hand, is dominated by much younger people. Because the movement is widespread and decentralized, it is difficult to get an overall set of reliable statistics. As well, the strong support of unions adds a higher number of older people to the mix. Nevertheless, studies as of the end of 2011 do confirm that Occupy is a movement of the millennials more than of any other age group.

- A November 2011 survey of over 5,000 visitors to the occupywallstreet.org website, reported by FastCompany.com, revealed that 23.5% of supporters were 24 years old or younger, and 44% were ages 25 to 44. Only 32% were 45 and older (vs. 70% for the Tea Party Express and 61% for the electorate as a whole)

- Another survey, undertaken by Baruch College of Public Affairs, polled Occupy supporters in New York's Zuccotti Park. The age break was 64% under 34, and only 20% over the age of 45

- A third survey, conducted by pollster Douglas Schoen in the same park, gave an age breakdown as follows.

Age Group Participation in Occupy Movement	
Ages	Percentage
18-29	49%
30-39	23%
40-49	15%
50-64	9%
65+	4%
65+	22%

I think it's fair, therefore, to contrast the Tea Party and Occupy as examples of how our two groups operate in the political world.

Before demonstrating just how striking that contrast is – and how unfavorable to the millennials – I want to emphasize that for the purposes of conducting this case study, I am deliberately not evaluating the merit of the aims or goals of the two groups. I am assuming that those aims or goals are, in both cases, good or valid or correct or any other complimentary adjective you might wish to use. The case study is not about the rightness or wrongness of what either the Tea Party movement or the Occupy movement is after. My only concern is how effective they are in the pursuit of those goals.

Tea Partiers, Occupiers, and Strategy

I think is accurate to say that the Tea Party has been, by orders of magnitude, more effective.

From its beginnings in early 2009, the Tea Party has swiftly become a force to be reckoned with in the Republican Party. On election day in November 2010, the Tea Party was able to materially influence the outcome of more than 200 federal and state elections. In the Republican primaries of 2012, all candidates are carefully weighing Tea Party reaction to the positions they take. This is not to say that the Tea Party can or will totally control the outcome of the Republican selection process, much less the outcome of the 2012 Presidential election. Nevertheless, they have become a powerful group, particularly at the state and local levels, where the work they do gains less media coverage but is nonetheless of tremendous influence on society.

The Occupy movement started about two years later, and, as I write, its initial demonstrations have all more or less ended. Supporters claim the Occupy movement has at least succeeded in changing the public debate by heightening awareness of income inequality. This has yet to be proved in the political arena, and there is not yet any evidence that the movement has been able to translate its ardor into meaningful political influence.

Looking at the two campaigns strictly in terms of strategy, organization, and behavior toward established political mechanisms, it is easy to see how and why the Tea Party movement has been more effective.

1. The Tea Party has clear, straightforward, and tightly focused goals. The Occupy movement does not.

2. Supporters and critics alike acknowledge the Tea Party has always had specific policy objectives and has developed means to achieve those objectives – that its focus is not on the conduct of the Tea Party supporters themselves. In the case of the Occupy movement, the reverse is true. Virtually all of the discussion that it generated quickly moved off its central complaint (financial inequality) and on to the behavior that prevailed at the various local Occupy events. This behavior ranged from the benign but weird (the human mic technique by which a speaker or discussion leader offered a phrase or sentence and the group immediately echoed it verbatim), to much more serious issues – dirt, disease, destruction of public property, and crime.

3. The Tea Party had a focused and defined strategy of working through the established political system and of taking control of a political party where that control could most easily be won – locally. The Occupy movement, by contrast, has no discernible strategy for bringing about the outcome it claims to desire (not that it is easy to discern what that outcome would be in the first place).

Contrast, for example, the home pages of the Tea Party Express and Occupy Wall Street, the originator of the Occupy movement.

Neither website is necessarily a triumph of graphics, but the differences in strategy are immediately discernible – and stark. The Tea Party states its objectives up front, in unmistakable language:

> *The Tea Party Express is proud to stand for six simple principles*
> - *No more bailouts*
> - *Reduce the size and intrusiveness of government*
> - *Stop raising our taxes*
> - *Repeal Obamacare*

- *Cease out-of-control spending*
- *Bring back American prosperity*

Except for the final item, all of these objectives can be translated into concrete political action. Candidates can – and did – pledge to base their legislative votes on meeting these demands. Indeed, the presence of a very committed sub-group of Republican Congressmen, who were elected in 2010 on the basis of Tea Party endorsement, has been seen as a major stumbling block to reaching any Republican-Democrat consensus on how to deal with the enormous debt burden of the federal government.

To be sure, the Tea Party has attracted an enormous amount of strident (and sometimes hysterical) criticism. But the criticism has almost always been aimed at what the Tea Party believes and what it wants to do, not on how its members have comported themselves in pursuing its ends. Except for one or two half-hearted attempts, at the very beginning, to portray Tea Party rallies as racist, there have been virtually no negative headlines about its conduct. Tea Party rallies did not involve the occupation of any public spaces. Tea Party members obtained permits, assembled, talked, and were careful to clean up after themselves. In other words, they created no distractions from their main message.

Now look at the Occupy Wall Street website, and ask yourself if it looks like the work of an organization that actually expects to achieve its goals. And by way, what are those goals? Try to find them. The best I could find was this paragraph in the right-hand column:

> **Occupy Wall Street** *is a leaderless resistance movement with people of many colors, genders and political persuasions. The one thing we all have in common is that We Are The 99% that will no longer tolerate the greed and corruption of the 1%. We are using the revolutionary Arab Spring tactic to achieve our ends and encourage the*

use of nonviolence to maximize the safety of all participants.

This #ows movement empowers real people to create real change from the bottom up. We want to see a general assembly in every backyard, on every street corner because we don't need Wall Street and we don't need politicians to build a better society.

The only solution is World Revolution

Could anything more perfectly represent the difference between boomers and seniors, on the one hand, and millennials, on the other? Let's parse some of the text, staying away from any critique of the underlying motivation (that the greed and corruption of the 1% represent an intolerable burden on the 99%).

"Occupy Wall Street is a leaderless resistance movement with people of many colors, genders and political persuasions."
Talk about throwing in your hand before you even start. If it's a leaderless movement, how does it expect to get anything done? Or perhaps it doesn't expect to. Is it enough to feel good about making the gesture? That would tie in perfectly with what the millennials have been taught all their lives.

"We are using the revolutionary Arab Spring tactic to achieve our ends and encourage the use of nonviolence to maximize the safety of all participants."
Numerous commentators have been scathing in their ridicule of this equation of conditions in the USA with the tyrannies of the Arab world. But our issue is: Can this possibly work? Is it likely that the wider audience would take this even remotely seriously? What's more, Arab Spring demonstrators such as those in Tahrir Square had an extremely narrow and focused objective – the removal of the dictator. One item only. Is there any such clarity in the Occupy Wall Street screed? As for nonviolence, how does this square with the clenched fist logo and the slogan that the "only solution is world revolution"?

"We want to see a general assembly in every backyard, on every street corner because we don't need Wall Street and we don't need politicians to build a better society. The only solution is World Revolution."

This passage could almost be a satire on the whole feelings-trump-substance mishmash in which the millennials grew up. Don't need politicians? Fine – then who is going to pass the laws that will reform things? And what would those laws *be*, come to think of it? And can anyone argue with a straight face that the "only" solution is *world* revolution? To the Tea Party, the solution was to try to take over the Republican Party one precinct at a time. Which seems more likely to work? Which approach has worked?

But perhaps the Wall Street contingent is uniquely impractical. As a crosscheck, I visited another Occupy website – the one in Toronto, where I live.

Here it was even harder to find a set of objectives, much less any idea of how to achieve those objectives. The closest I could find was this:

> *Occupy Toronto is a peaceful grassroots movement that is fed up with the current political and economic systems in this nation and all over the world. We are an independent branch from the movement that started with the Occupation of Wall Street but we endorse the same values and philosophy. We have come together to find solutions to the difficulties we are facing in society today. We have not yet put out a unified message but be sure it will come.*
>
> *Occupy Toronto is a movement that intends to show its solidarity with the Occupy Wall Street and European Indignated movements. We stand in unity with the rest of the world to seek and work towards drastic changes to economic systems that are destroying our business, social liberties, and environment. We are, through entirely*

non-violent means, sending a message to the financial sector worldwide that banks exist to serve us, not the other way around, that the practices of speculation and fractional reserve lending have created a massive inequality and are no longer valid systems.

Current monetary policies enacted through globalization and privatization are unacceptably harming the majority. Monetary policy should be created to help these very people. Our target is to change these systems to help the 99% of the population, instead of just the elite 1% that they currently benefit. Everyone is encouraged to join the movement, this movement affects us all.

But if the specific goals are unstated, never mind the policies that would need to be enacted to achieve them, the same could not be said about the activities of the group. They were busy, busy, busy. The website was packed with news of committees, gatherings, subsets of the experience. There were no fewer than 22 groups meeting regularly, and in some cases even posting minutes – Fundraising, Minutes, Arts and Culture, Facilitation, Web Development, Direct Action, Offsite, Livestream, Legal, Outreach, Content Editors, Winterization, Sustainability, Press Relations, Info Desk, Action Committee, Visual Media, Newspaper, Food, and Logistics.

Fine – but in the service of *what*? What were they meeting *about*? What were they actually *doing*? Almost in desperation, on November 24, 2011, I clicked on the Action Committee. Surely this was where I could get some concrete information. Here is what I read:

> *The Action Committee meets every weekday at the action tent (near Info), at 8:30 in the evening. Our Monday and Thursday meetings are our big decision making meetings, while our Tuesday, wed* [sic]*, and Friday meetings are more for pre-planning and smaller actions.*

Actions include anything from rallies, large marches, organized responses to eviction, creative and artistic direct actions, etc ...

Actions are the bread and butter of this movement, so get involved and lets [sic] *fight for the change we want to see!*

On the very same day, here is what I found on the website of the Tea Party Express:

- A petition that visitors could sign, telling the Super Committee of the US Congress (who by then had failed to agree on spending cuts) to cut spending and not raise taxes
- The naming of four Senators that the Tea Party was targeting for defeat in the 2012 elections – Olympia Snowe of Maine, Richard Lugar of Indiana, Ben Nelson of Nebraska, and Debby Stabenow of Michigan. (Interestingly, Snow and Lugar are Republicans)
- A solicitation to join the e-mail list
- A video featuring Amy Kremer, Chair of the Tea Party Express
- Links to two years' worth of press releases endorsing, or opposing, candidates at the national and local levels
- A link to the Tea Party Express blog
- Links to Tea Party presence on Facebook and Twitter
- Links to a Tea Party Express video featuring a campaign rally in New Hampshire with Herman Cain
- Links to the Tea Party Express radio hour (broadcast every Monday night) and to several podcasts
- Links to a Tea Party Express store, selling apparel, mugs, calendars, and more

Yes, it's obvious that the Tea Party could be expected to have produced more. As of November 2011, they had been around for more than two years, whereas the Occupy movement had been in action for only three months or so. Maybe so, but it's also obvious that the Tea Party is the more serious organization. They are focused on more concrete goals, and they have identified specific actions to achieve those goals. They're also adept at using the digital and social media tools, something identified more with millennials than with the older generations.

It's very clear, when you study the two movements, that the Tea Party is concerned with results and the Occupy movement with a feel-good experience that validates its participants. Unfortunately, this experience quickly degenerated – although not in all locations – into a very unattractive mixture of squalor, uncouth behavior, and frequent violence.

In fact, most of the public attention quickly turned to the conduct of the Occupy movement, and not to its critique of society or its objectives, such as they were. Vandalism, assaults, even arson and rape, were reported at more than one location. A YouTube video showed an Occupy organizer in Baltimore suggesting that rape victims not report anything to the police. In Oakland, stores that quickly posted signs saying they supported the Occupy movement had their windows broken and merchandise stolen anyway.

At almost all locations, public debate also quickly centered on whether the Occupy protesters should be allowed to, well, *occupy*. If the average person couldn't set up a tent and occupy a public park, why should the Occupy forces be allowed to do so? Did their freedom of speech trump the rights of citizens to use public squares and parks and not see them trashed? An interesting question, to be sure – but for that very reason, one that quickly overshadowed the actual cause the Occupy movement claimed it represented. The validity of that cause was lost in the debate about behavior.

The Tea Party, by contrast, has not allowed the conduct of its demonstrations to become the topic. It has kept the focus

– even in the minds of critics – on the policies it advocates. It has also aligned its strategy and its desired outcome, working within the conventional political system to influence the selection of candidates, who, once nominated, had a good chance to win, and who, once elected, would vote for measures supported by the Tea Party.

On the Occupy side, there is no such connection between desired goals, policies that would achieve those goals, and actions that could bring those policies into force in the real world. It is all make-believe.

The contrast perfectly reflects the different natures of the competing generations.

A relentless focus on desired outcome, executed with a mixture of realism (figure out how things work and use that knowledge to your advantage) and discipline, has always been characteristic of the boomers and the immediate pre-boomers, if not the oldest seniors.

The millennials, in contrast, have always been much less inclined to do the hard work of figuring out how to produce concrete results. Why should they? Their education has put a premium on rewards detached from results. The need to foster self-esteem, the need to make sure nobody was without a prize, the dilution of standards so that everyone would be an achiever – and, in case of difficulty, the problem would be fixed by helicopter parents – these influences were bound to produce what the Occupy movement quickly became.

One strong proof of this can be found in the advice that was tendered in November 2011 by *Adbusters*, the Canadian magazine that was one of the major influences in the creation of the Occupy movement in the first place.

Winter was imminent. More and more occupiers were being evicted. The movement was being subjected to increasingly strong criticism, even by those who had started out as supporters, for its lack of clear objectives, lack of policy ideas, and tolerance of anti-social (and at times, criminal) behavior.

Here's what *Adbusters* said, under the heading *Tactical Briefing #18*:

Hey you creatives, artists, environmentalists, workers, moms, dads, students, malcontents, do-gooders and aspiring martyrs in the snow:
The last four months have been hard fought, inspiring and delightfully revolutionary. We brought tents, hunkered down, held our assemblies, and lobbed a meme-bomb that continues to explode the world's imagination. Many of us have never felt so alive. We have fertilized the future with our revolutionary spirit ... and a thousand flowers will surely bloom in the coming Spring.

But as winter approaches an ominous mood could set in ... hope thwarted is in danger of turning sour, patience exhausted becoming anger, militant nonviolence losing its allure. It isn't just the mainstream media that says things could get ugly. What shall we do to keep the magic alive?

Here are a couple of emerging ideas:

STRATEGY #1: We summon our strength, grit our teeth and hang in there through winter ... heroically we sleep in the snow ... we impress the world with our determination and guts ... and when the cops come, we put our bodies on the line and resist them nonviolently with everything we've got.

STRATEGY #2: We declare "victory" and throw a party ... a festival ... a potlatch ... a jubilee ... a grand gesture to celebrate, commemorate, rejoice in how far we've come, the comrades we've made, the glorious days ahead. Imagine, on a Saturday yet to be announced, perhaps our movement's three month anniversary on December 17, in every #OCCUPY in the world, we reclaim the streets for a weekend of triumphant hilarity and joyous revelry.

We dance like we've never danced before and invite the world to join us.

What's interesting here is the complete detachment from the actual cause and the relentless focus on how the participants are feeling *about themselves*. The issue they claim to have been motivated by – greed, corruption, wealth inequality – is nowhere to be found. Why? Because *how they feel* is more important. After all, as they put it, "we brought tents, hunkered down, held our assemblies and lobbed a meme-bomb." A meme-bomb, no less. Aren't they entitled to feel wonderful? And they do. "Many of us have never felt so alive."

But negative feelings threaten to intrude. "An ominous mood could set in." Hope could turn sour, and patience, "exhausted," could morph into anger. And so the question is posed: "What should we do to keep the magic alive?"

The question is significant because it revolves on mood, feelings, and attitudes and not on results. *Adbusters* doesn't ask, "What have we accomplished? What allies have we made? What proposals have we put forward that have a chance of being adopted? What are the next steps if we really want to accomplish something?" Instead, the focus is the demonstrators themselves and their need to sustain an atmosphere.

The two strategic options reflect this. The first – "hang in there through the winter" – is a possibility not because it will get the movement closer to any tangible *outcome* but because it will "impress the world with our determination and guts." The focus is on the demonstrators again, and not what they are trying to achieve (to the extent that a concrete outcome can even be discerned).

The second option is even more telling: "We declare 'victory' and throw a party ... a festival ... a potlatch ... a jubilee ... a grand gesture to celebrate ..." This distills in a sentence the entire social and educational experience of the millennial generation. Win or lose, everyone must be validated, everyone must win a prize. So they are to "rejoice in how far we've come, the comrades we've made, the glorious days ahead ..." The definition of success shifts from achieving social or political goals to sustaining a feel-good experience. It is almost impossible to exaggerate the infantilism on display here.

The boomers and seniors, by contrast, have no such stars in their eyes. Smack-dab in the middle of the whole Occupy happening, the AARP continued to run a TV commercial in which a senior citizen cold-bloodedly reminds politicians of where the votes are. Here is a storyboard of the message. As you read it, compare the message with that of the Occupy movement. Assume the stated goals of both groups are equally laudable and ask yourself which group, and which message, has the better chance of being actualized in the real world.

AARP Commercial: Where the Votes Are

I'm not a number.
I'm not a line item on a budget.

And I'm definitely not a pushover.
But I am a voter.

So Washington, before you even think about cutting my Medicare and my Social Security benefits...

...here's a number you should remember. Fifty million. We are fifty million seniors who earned our benefits

...and you will be hearing from us. Today – and on election day.

Look at the closing frame with its focused and concrete "ask" – CUT WASTE AND LOOPHOLES, NOT OUR BENEFITS. An ask that is achievable in the real world, an achievement linked directly to the other part of the message – 50 million voters. There is not an atom of fluff or illusion here; it's strictly business.

The boomers and seniors are taking their problems seriously; the millennials are content with righteous indignation and feel-good posturing.

But surely I'm being unfair. After all, the boomers and seniors have, by definition, decades of more experience than the millennials. They know how the system works and how to work the system. They've also seen revolutionary fervor crash on the rocks of messy reality. Of course they're more effective; they're bound to be. Surely I am making a federal case out of the very natural and normal difference between maturity and immaturity.

In a universal sense, this is so. Every generation comes into adulthood thinking it has all the answers; every older generation rolls its eyes and says, "Yeah, sure, kid." The Occupy demonstrators of today will one day be grandparents and great-grandparents and will tut-tut over whatever the youth of that era come up with and will remember (with mixed feelings, no doubt) their own youthful fire-in-the-belly.

But beyond this truism, there is something much deeper and more serious here, something that particularly relates to the boomers. Of course you'd expect them, in their 50s or early 60s, to be more effective than the millennials. But what's also true is that they were more effective *even when they were the same age the millennials are now.*

Look at the big causes that the boomers adopted when they were in university or just coming out of university. Civil rights. The Vietnam War. Or if you want a Canadian example, Trudeaumania. What the boomers went after, they got.

They did so by doing everything the millennials are not

doing. They were focused in what they were pursuing, and what they were pursuing was possible. Extending civil rights to African-Americans, or ending the Vietnam War, were specific and concrete objectives that could be – and were – achieved within the existing political system. Same for electing Pierre Elliott Trudeau.

The boomers also showed tremendous patience and staying power and were much more realistic and tough-minded about what it would take to achieve the desired outcomes. Those who marched for civil rights in the Deep South faced real physical threats – even death – and had to show great courage in the face of repeated setbacks. (Most, to be fair, were four or five years older than the oldest baby boomers, but that simply extends my point to cover seniors. Michael Schwerner, who was murdered in Mississippi in 1964, would be 72 years old today.) Recalling their heroism, and then reading the self-indulgent faux-martyr verbiage in the *Adbusters* Tactical Briefing #18 ("… when the cops come, we put our bodies on the line and resist them non-violently with everything we've got"), you have to squirm in embarrassment for the millennials.

But maybe you think I'm editorializing a bit here, letting some of my own political prejudices creep in. So let me nail down the point by invoking the Students for a Democratic Society.

SDS was the leading radical left-wing student activist group in the USA in the 1960s. It started life as the youth branch of a socialist organization called the League for Industrial Democracy before spinning off under a separate name in 1960. In 1962, it issued its famous political manifesto, known as the Port Huron Statement.

SDS was considered on the extreme left. For example, while not being Marxist or pro-communist, it attacked anti-communism as being anti-democratic and allowed delegates from Communist youth organizations to attend its conferences. (More mainline left-wing organizations, out of fears born in the McCarthy era, always professed their anti-communism.) SDS also eventually spun off an even more radical group, the Weather Underground, which advocated violence and carried out several bombings.

I mention all this only to establish the radical credentials of the organization. If any group could be expected to merchandise extreme solutions or engage in simplistic sloganeering, you would think it would be they.

But the Port Huron Statement, written by Tom Hayden, runs to over 30 pages of detailed, tightly reasoned, highly sophisticated argument built on objective evidence. The document shows a tremendous respect for the intelligence of its audience. Raw idealism or purity of motives are not presented as sufficient to carry the day. It is assumed the audience requires facts, logic, and an action plan with a reasonable chance to succeed.

I will present just a few excerpts – and remember, these words were written in 1962, and these were the radicals of the day. As you read these passages, ask yourself if you could even remotely imagine such work being produced by the Occupy movement.

Theoretic chaos has replaced the idealistic thinking of old – and, unable to reconstitute theoretic order, men have condemned idealism itself. Doubt has replaced hopefulness – and men act out a defeatism that is labelled realistic. The decline of utopia and hope is in fact one of the defining features of social life today. The reasons are various: the dreams of the older left were perverted by Stalinism and never recreated; the congressional stalemate makes men narrow their view of the possible; the specialization of human activity leaves little room for sweeping thought; the horrors of the twentieth century, symbolized by the gas-ovens and concentration camps and atom bombs, have blasted hopefulness. To be idealistic is to be considered apocalyptic, deluded. To have no serious aspirations, on the contrary, is to be "toughminded."

Another example:

The civil rights struggle ... has come to an impasse. To this impasse, the movement responded this year by entering the sphere of politics, insisting on citizenship rights, specifically the right to vote. The new voter registration stage of protest represents perhaps the first major attempt to exercise the conventional instruments of political democracy in the struggle for racial justice. The vote, if used strategically by the great mass of now-unregistered Negroes theoretically eligible to vote, will be a decisive factor in changing the quality of Southern leadership from low demagoguery to decent statesmanship ...

Linked with pressure from Northern liberals to expunge the Dixiecrats from the ranks of the Democratic Party, massive Negro voting in the South could destroy the vice-like grip reactionary Southerners have on the Congressional legislative process.

And finally, this:

Social relevance, the accessibility to knowledge and internal openness – these together make the university a potential base and agency in a movement of social change.

1. *Any new left in America must be, in large measure, a left with real intellectual skills, committed to deliberativeness, honesty, reflection as working tools. The university permits the political life to be an adjunct to the academic one, and action to be informed by reason.*

2. *A new left must be distributed in significant social roles throughout the country. The universities are distributed in such a manner.*

3. *A new left must consist of younger people who matured in the postwar world, and partially be*

directed to the recruitment of younger people. The university is an obvious beginning point.

4. *A new left must include liberals and socialists, the former for their relevance, the latter for their sense of thoroughgoing reforms in the system. The university is a more sensible place than a political party for these two traditions to begin to discuss their differences and look for political synthesis.*

5. *A new left must start controversy across the land, if national politics and national apathy are to be reverse. The ideal university is a community of controversy, within itself and in its effects on communities beyond.*

6. *... In a time of supposed prosperity, moral complacency and political manipulation, a new left cannot rely on only aching stomachs to be the engine force for social reform. The case for change, for alternatives that will involve uncomfortable personal efforts, must be argued as never before. The university is a relevant place for all of these activities.*

Tom Hayden was born in 1939, six or seven years ahead of the baby boom. Today, at 72, he's a senior. He was only 23 when he wrote this, and the oldest boomer today was at that time 17. Within five years, boomers and pre-boomers had coalesced into a powerful force for social change, with the universities as their base, exactly as Hayden had advocated. (I am not suggesting that Hayden originated this idea; it had been voiced by many others, and much earlier, and in some ways echoes Marxist philosopher Antonio Gramsci's exhortations about the "long march through the institutions.") Hayden was also prescient in his predictions about the positive outcomes of black voting rights and the ending of the "vice-like grip reactionary Southerners have on the Congressional legislative process."

But more than the accuracy of his predictions, or the validity of his ideology and proposed actions, consider simply the depth and sophistication of this work. There was little or no room for feel-good rhetoric; while Hayden was bold in declaring how the ideals of the new left could transform America for the good, he never allowed that vision to be detached from the harder questions of just how these goals could be realized. Ambitious goals, yes – but there was no prize for the ambition; the prize would come when the goals were achieved.

And many of those goals were achieved. The pre-boomers and boomers drove Lyndon Johnson from office and saw the end of the Vietnam War (and made sure it would be seen as a failure ever after). They saw the enactment of sweeping civil rights legislation, and a revolution in black political power. (Hayden himself was a Freedom Rider in Mississippi and was arrested and beaten.) As a generation, they got much of what they were after.

They worked largely through the established political system and the prevailing channels of communication and persuasion. They were persistent in the face of powerful opposition from older generations, but they were also effective in gradually mobilizing opinion from segments of those older generations, and working with those older supporters. Their patience was not exhausted after a couple of months – as *Adbusters* worried that of the Occupy participants would be. They did not declare victory and throw a party just to make everyone feel good about themselves.

Tom Hayden, incidentally, went on to a distinguished career in politics, writing, and advocacy. He has written 19 books and served 18 years in the California state legislature, where he was responsible for over 100 bills, ranging from children's health standards to reducing start-up fees for small businesses to funding for gang intervention projects to equal university access for disabled students. He served twice on the national platform committee of the Democratic Party and has taught at Scripps and Claremont College and the Harvard Institute of

Politics. (And if all that wasn't enough, he was also married for a time to Jane Fonda.)

Hayden's career is instructive for our purposes here, because it is an excellent example of how much more serious and goal-oriented seniors and boomers were, even when they were younger.

But surely not *all* of them. What about the hippies? What about the drug culture? What about "tune in, turn on, drop out"? What about the Weathermen? It's true: The pre-boomers and boomers who created the "if it feels good, do it" 1960s did include a lot of people who dressed the part and played at being radical but didn't really get anything done – or, in some cases, got bad things done.

Nevertheless, those generations have a sum total body of work to their credit and – at least in terms of achieving declared objectives – it is impressive. What's more, even with all the sideshows – bra-burning, drugs, free love – on the key issues there was a significant degree of focus, patience, determination, and skill. There were concrete goals and persistence in achieving those goals. The Flower Children who said "make love, not war" and put daisies down the barrels of the rifles of ROTC members on college campuses didn't lose patience and declare victory after three or so months. The pre-boomers and boomers were able to differentiate between form and substance. They certainly displayed radical behavior (compared with their parents) in the clothes they wore or their willingness to experiment with drugs and sex. But this didn't keep them from being hard-nosed and determined on the big social and political issues that motivated them – as is proven by, dare I use the word, the *results*.

It's also worth noting how many of these very same hippies morphed rather easily into the money-driven yuppies of the 1970s. They went through the dress-up phase and had a good time while still accomplishing (or at least heavily influencing) some serious goals, and then simply went after the next thing they wanted.

And so here we are today.

Just read the *Adbusters* column again and then take another look at that senior citizen in the AARP commercial. Or reread a passage from the Port Huron statement. Which generation is going to get what it wants, and which generation will be left writing resentful blog posts while awarding itself prizes for meme-bombs?

But those are the easy questions with obvious answers. And perhaps it is unfair to expect more from the millennials (even though, as I have shown, the boomers at the same age as the millennials were much more effective).

The more important question is, Where are the solutions going to come from? Which generation will create the peace? And – beyond the peace – which will lay the groundwork for a more constructive post-war era?

Surprise, surprise ...

10
The Boomers Take Action

*T*o this point, many readers may think I have not offered much evidence that the war of the generations metaphor is all that inappropriate. They may think that while the language associated with intergenerational conflict is sometimes overheated, it is nevertheless true that there *is* a competition for scarce resources, and it really is pitting boomers and seniors against millennials.

Of course, I acknowledge this – not as a concession, but as a necessary condition for carrying the discussion further. The reason I object to the war metaphor, the reason I conclude that it is largely a myth, is *not* to deny the presence of competing wants and needs associated with increased longevity – and, even more acutely, increased longevity in the case of the boomers. It is fatuous to believe that we can materially extend the human life span, and accompany that extension with significant attitude changes that destroy previous notions of expected behaviors associated with aging, and *not* trigger a cascade of effects on all generations, particularly the younger ones who are emerging into adulthood just as the older folks are reinventing and reconfiguring their own identities. What else could we expect but a clash of expectations? Why should we be surprised that it is accompanied by strong feelings of uncertainty and even antipathy? I am trying to make it clear, at the outset of this chapter, that my objections to the war metaphor do not derive from a desire to sugarcoat the realities of intergenerational competition. No, what makes the war metaphor a myth is the simple fact that, even as the struggle is going on, *one of the forces is already fighting for the other side.*

Before I lay out the evidence, let's review what we have come to see so far.

There is a natural and understandable conflict between many of the key needs and wants of the boomers and seniors, on the one hand, and those of the millennials, on the other. This conflict is most acute in the job market; it is somewhat more indirect, although still serious, in areas of public policy where a squeeze on government resources puts pressure on big-spending categories, intensifying the competition for scarce dollars.

On the jobs front, the boomers, from a combination of need and attitude, are not retiring on schedule. The 2008 financial wipeout made this trend stronger – and even drew many retired seniors back into the workforce. The result was to put serious barriers in the path of millennials trying to enter the job market for the first time.

On the public policy front, boomers and seniors are fighting hard to preserve health-care and pension entitlements, and this is bound to conflict with some of the needs of the millennials, most notably when it comes to government spending on education and policies to relieve student debt levels. On this battleground, the millennials face large and well-organized lobby groups – backed by the voting power of the boomers and seniors – that will do everything they can to make sure politicians preserve (or even increase) their hard-won benefits.

As we've also seen, this conflict has produced a significant level of Age Rage. The angry millennials blame the greedy boomers: Why won't they step out of the way and give the younger generations a chance? Why won't they cut back on their entitlement demands in order to leave a few pennies on the table for someone else? In terms of rhetoric, Age Rage is very real.

But the boomers have thick skins. They've spent a lifetime, after all, being excoriated by everyone ... including more than a few of their own generation. So they push back: The millennials are whiners, the millennials have no work ethic, the millennials are softies who don't know how to deal with adversity. Who told them to borrow money for degrees in soft subjects that don't lead to jobs? They should stop sniveling, stop behaving like the entitlement generation, grow up, and get on with it. The boomers – let's face it – are quite capable of making their own strong contribution to Age Rage.

But they're not stopping there. Even as they are fighting aggressively for their own interests, they are already mounting a rescue operation for the millennials. A Marshall Plan, if you will, one that isn't waiting until after the surrender ceremony but is quietly (and sometimes not so quietly) being put into place even now.

A Boomer Marshall Plan

The millennials will be saved – by their opponents in the so-called war of the generations.

Not that the older folks – particularly the boomers – will be entirely thrilled about it. Not that they won't have some editorial comment to offer along the way (a different version of Age Rage). But when push comes to shove, the boomers, as they have been all along, will continue to be the grownups, and continue to pay the bills. They aren't decommissioning those helicopters any time soon. Even as they continue to lobby aggressively for their own benefits and entitlements – no let-up on that front – they are a beacon of support for their lost-at-sea kids.

And they're doing it – in typical boomer fashion – by turning their efforts into a new component of their own identity.

Just as they have reinvented aging, so they are now reinventing parenting.

Of course, the underlying reasons include cold-blooded pragmatism. Just as the Marshall Plan rested on cost/benefit analysis as well as on morality (turning bombed-out, poverty-stricken Europeans into future consumers of American products), so the boomers, even as they continue to clog the job market and protect their benefits and entitlements, have calculated that if they don't shore up their kids now, those kids may be on the payroll for keeps.

But it's not enough to grumble and furtively fork over a few dollars now and then. Boomers being boomers, the process is being elevated – to a cause, to a trend, to a reinvention of past norms. This is happening from the top down, and from the bottom up.

Boomers Assisting from the Top Down

From the top down, it's being framed, by the usual suspects, as a moral imperative. It is being called for by an increasingly large number of (real or self-declared) thinkers and pundits, particularly guilt-ridden boomers.

Helping the younger generation is "the least we can do," says *The Atlantic* in an extensive feature on this topic in October 2010. A long article by Michael Kinsley leads the way, with a spirited follow-on discussion by a number of other real or self-declared experts. The intro to the piece sets the tone.

> *Self-absorbed, self-indulged, and self-loathing, the baby Boom generation at last has the chance to step out of the so-called Greatest Generation's historical shadow. Boomers may not have the opportunity to save the world, as their predecessors did, but they can still redeem themselves by saving the American economy*

from the fiscal mess that they, and their fathers and mothers, are leaving behind.

After an intro like this, the slant comes as no surprise. Kinsley does makes a nod at being impartial, noting that "the indictment against the Baby Boomer generation is familiar, way oversimplified, and only partly fair." But then he goes on to tell us how he really feels: The Boomers ran up huge debt while trashing the image of America. "Things are generally going to hell."

Is there a remedy for this? Yes. Is it too late? No. The boomers can at last redeem the mess they have made of everything.

It's not too late for a generational gesture, something that will be the equivalent of – if not actually equal to – our parents' sacrifice in fighting and winning World War II: some act of generosity or sacrifice that will inspire or embarrass the next generation, as the sacrifices and achievements of the "Greatest" generation inspire and embarrass many Boomers. So what'll it be, folks?

Kinsley's answer is cash.

We should pass on to the next generation an America that's free from debt. Instead of ignoring it, or arguing endlessly about whose fault it is and who should pay for it, Boomers as an age cohort should just grab the check and say, "This one's on us."

"This one's on us"? Kinsley estimates that about $14 trillion would need to be raised. But hey, no problem. The money could be accumulated through a combination of estate taxes and voluntary contributions, "our generation's once-in-a-lifetime parting gift to those who follow."

That's some "parting gift," but Kinsley is untroubled. In fact, it's not as big a gift as the greedy boomers have received from their parents. "Boomers could forswear all or part of this unearned inheritance. Or, more realistically, they could allow the government to tax it."

Kinsley points out that the tax rate wouldn't even be that high, given the huge amount of money the boomers are going to inherit; even a relatively modest collection of 20% would throw off $8 trillion, he says. He notes that critics of the estate tax say it's a double tax – once when the income is earned, and once again when whatever is left over is passed along in the estate. Big deal. The boomers may be paying twice, he concedes, "but that's the idea. That's what you do because you didn't have to fight in World War II." Which brings us back to the subtitle of the piece, which included "self-loathing" as a boomer attribute.

I'm not sure why Kinsley feels guilty about not having fought in World War II – he wasn't born until 1951 – but his guilt takes him even further. He suggests the boomers give back the unused portion of the money their parents have received from Social Security. He suggests this could, with enough peer pressure, become "a social norm."

And, now that we're on a roll, why stop there? Why not refuse to receive those oh-so-expensive medical treatments that prolong your life if you're very old? In this way the boomers not only can free up the cash to save the system, but can do so through a retroactive and reverse Omaha Beach in which they can *die while carrying out the rescue*. "Just a thought," Kinsley says.

Kinsley is smart enough to realize that the logical question is what's stopping him from doing this himself – from "walking around with a permanent Do Not Resuscitate order" tattooed on his chest. His answer: "*I'm not doing this alone. That would not achieve the purpose of vindicating a generation. Anyway, democratic government is a way of saying 'I will if you will.'*"

The Atlantic carried a number of follow-on pieces that found plenty of material to praise or deride. One of the strongest voices was that of Lisa Chamberlain, author of *Slackonomics: Generation X in the Age of Creative Destruction*. She stepped up as the voice of the generation following the boomers, a generation she describes as the boomers' "clean-up crew":

> Baby Boomers will not be rushing to raise taxes on themselves, as Michael Kinsley proposes they do to save America's fiscal future, but sooner or later they are going to be out of the picture and the reality of today's economy will have to be dealt with – and that reality is much more familiar to Generation X than the Boomers.

She's not impressed by Kinsley's effort to "convince his fellow Boomers to fulfill the promise of their generation by saving the economy for the next generation." While noting that it is "a commendable thought," she observes that it is also "like most Boomer ideas, totally unrealistic." The real answers will be found among the Gen Xers, she declares:

> So enough about boomers – no, really, enough about the Boomers – what about us Gen Xers, the real clean-up crew? While social upheaval and world wars marked previous generations in their formative years, the boom-and-bust economy has been defining the Gen X experience from the moment we entered the labor force.

In other words, the very forces that are provoking such Age Rage among the millennials are old hat to Generation X.

> There is no question that the overarching influence on Generation X has been enduring economic whiplash, a condition that continues unabated in this hyperactive era of "creative destruction," defined by the contradictory forces of economic insecurity on the one hand and the unleashing of human potential as a result of advanced technology on the other. The downside of this condition is that Gen Xers tend to be highly individualistic and not prone to collective action. The good news is, it's made us highly practical and not prone to ideological dogmatism.

We could have taken a very enjoyable detour into the idea that Gen Xers received, in a way, an appetizer for the main course of economic ruin that was heaped on the millennials, and that this has made them tougher and more capable than the entitlement generation. But all I want to establish is that there is a very substantial body of top-down hortatory work calling on the boomers to mend their sinful ways, if only for the sake of not passing from the scene in utter disgrace.

And come to think of it, this rationale may simply be a demonstration of understanding one's audience and what will motivate it.

Boomers Assisting from the Bottom Up

There is a lot more action, however, that is bottom-up – the real actions of millions of individuals, motivated largely by immediate and very pragmatic issues. True (and in typical boomer fashion), these actions have been quickly rolled up into new trends, complete with the usual array of books, seminars, and websites – and we'll certainly take a look at all of that. But first let's just lay out the dollars and cents.

The picture is clear. In both Canada and the USA, baby boomers (and to some extent, seniors) are providing significant financial help to their adult children or grandchildren, and in some cases have rearranged their own financial plans and priorities, particularly with respect to housing and retirement.

A 2010 survey for the Investors Group, "Boomers on Call," showed that 6 out of 10 boomers were providing financial support to adult children, with an average amount of $3,675 per year. And this was on top of providing some financial support to aging parents (10% of boomers were contributing) and trying to manage their own requirements and save for retirement. While they didn't mind helping their own moms and dads (66% said they thought of this as a repayment for what their parents had done for them), 25% said they weren't all that happy about still needing to provide financial help to their kids – although this unhappiness didn't stop them from doing it.

These findings are consistent with data from the USA. For example, a survey conducted in May 2011 for the National Endowment for Financial Education, in cooperation with *Forbes* magazine, found that 59% of parents were providing or had provided financial help for adult children who were no longer in school. They were supporting the children in a variety of ways:

- 50% were providing housing
- 48% were helping with living expenses
- 41% were contributing to transportation costs
- 35% were helping with insurance coverage
- 29% were providing spending money
- 28% were kicking in funds for medical bills

Other US-based surveys reveal similar data. In a 2011 survey for VibrantNation.com, an online community for women over the age of 50, over 80% of respondents said they were paying more bills for their adult children than their parents had paid for them. Almost 60% were paying cell-phone bills, and over a third were paying for or subsidizing items such as rent, clothes, or cars. And in yet another 2011 survey, this one for *Better Homes and Gardens*, one in five baby boomers said they had paid, loaned, or co-signed a loan to help their children or grandchildren buy a home. And two-thirds said they'd be very interested in doing so in the future.

The motivation for helping the kids get their own place is obvious: The percentage of adult children still living with their parents is at an all-time high.

This is a dramatic trend, as may also be seen in a 2011 Statistics Canada report that compares and contrasts boomers, Gen Xers, and millennials as they were or are between the ages of 20 and 29. The report studies three groups: "Late Boomers" (born between 1957 and 1966); "Generation X" (born between 1969 and 1978); and "Millennials" (born between 1981 and 1990). Using those benchmarks, all three groups represent about the same number of people and the same split between ages 20 to 24 and ages 25 to 29. The report covers a wide range of topics; I've selected numbers that bear directly on what we're dealing with.

Late Boomers, Generation X, and Millennials Compared at Similar Stages			
	Late Boomers (1957-1966)	Generation X (1969-1978)	Millennials (1981-1990)
Number (000)	4,552	4,186	4,663
% ages 20-24	50	48	49
% Married or common-law	48	37	33
% with children	29	22	19
% living at home – Total	28	31	51
% living at home – ages 20-24	43	46	73
% living at home – ages 25-29	12	17	30

For all three groups, there is a dramatic drop-off in the percentage living at home once the age of 25 is reached. This is not surprising. Typically, a B.A. degree is not completed until age 22 or 23, so the bulk of kids 20 to 24 who are still living at home would have been students, and they would have moved out after finishing their education and entering the workforce.

Even so, only 43% of Late Boomers were living at home when they were 20 to 24 years old. Not much had changed by the time the Gen Xers hit that age: 46% were living at home. But look at the jump for the Millennials: 73% of those 20 to 24 were living at home, a 70% increase over the Late Boomer rate and a 59% increase over the Gen X rate.

Now look what happens in the 25 to 29 range. Only 12% of the Late Boomers were still living at home, and only 17% of the Gen Xers. But 30% of the Millennials are still under their parents' roof – more than double the rate of the Late Boomers and almost double that of the Gen Xers.

These numbers are consistent with US trends. In both countries, the impact on the boomers is not small.

In Canada, for example, as found in a survey by Forum Research for the *Financial Post*, two-thirds of adult children living at home were not paying rent or contributing to household expenses. Jonathan Chevreau, who writes the "Wealthy Boomer" column for the *Financial Post*, summed up some other key findings (November 2011):

> *If they had the option, a quarter of the parents would downsize their home or rent out part of it, were it not for the fact their adult kids were still living there. Roughly one in 10 parents anticipate postponing their retirement to accommodate their live-in children: 9% expect to delay retirement by two to five years and another 8% expect it to push off their retirement date by up to two years.*
>
> *The arrangement is also adding to the stress of parents, in addition to the financial toll. Less than a third said having a grown child at home didn't stress them at all and only 2% thought it lowered their stress. Some 38% thought it raised their stress "somewhat" and another 29% felt it did so "a great deal."*

In another survey released in November 2011 – this one by TD Canada Trust – about a third of boomers said they were planning to downsize, but of that total, almost 20% said they were delaying because they still had adult children in their 20s and even 30s still living at home.

Not surprisingly, this phenomenon of Boomerang Children has taken on all the trappings of a major trend – including the requisite books, self-seminars, websites, blogs, and social media groups. An Internet search for "Parenting your adult child" turns up almost 30 million results, many of them leading to self-help books such as the following.

The Hands-on Guide to Surviving Adult Children Living at Home has an interesting website promoting the tools offered in the book.

www.adultchildrenlivingathome.com

One of those tools is a customizable "under one roof" contract that helps parents set household rules, determines who covers what expenses, and addresses "the thorny issue" of overnight guests, chores, privacy rules, and more. There's also a household budget calculator to help boomer browsers determine the impact of their boomerang kids on their household budget.

Just for fun, I signed up for their free e-newsletter. I received in return a special report, "The 8 Most Dangerous Mistakes Parents Make When Their Adult Child Lives at Home." In case you're wondering, here they are:

1. *Encouraging rebellion by taking up parenting right where you left off*

2. *Letting anger and resentment destroy your relationship with your children*

3. *Stealing your child's independence by giving them a "free ride"*

4. *"We're all adults here, so there's no need for rules"*

5. *Assuming your adult child will leave when the time is right*

6. *Sacrificing your relationship with your spouse (this mistake is especially dangerous if the adult children are "steps")*

7. *Trampling your adult child's ability to be a good parent to their own children*

8. *Compromising your own financial situation – or even taking on a second job – to support your adult child and their family*

I found the list to be a reasonable mixture of "tough love" and compassion and wondered how the program was going and what the reactions had been. So I contacted Christina Newberry, the Vancouver-based writer and editor who created it. She agreed to an e-mail interview.

Q: *How did you come up with the idea to create this program?*

A: I boomeranged home twice – right after I finished university, at age 22, for about eight months, and then again at age 29, after the end of a relationship. The second time, I planned to stay for six months or so but realized quickly that living with my parents at that stage in my life was just not an ideal option for me, so I ended up staying for less than two months. So, my parents and I learned some lessons through both stays about what worked for us and what didn't, and what kinds of solutions we could come up with to fix some of the minor challenges so they didn't turn into major issues.

Meanwhile, I was developing a career in communications and management and realized that many of the techniques I had learned for goal-setting, performance reviews, and dealing with problem employee behavior would work well in the boomerang kid context, since most of the parent-child conflicts are a result of poor planning and communication or misaligned expectations.

Q: *What's been the response so far? Are you getting lots of positive comments? Any pushback from the adult kids?*

A: The response from parents has been excellent. In many cases, parents are happy just to know they are not alone in having problems adjusting to living with an adult child. Parents specifically say they find the contract template I offer to be the most helpful, as it forces them to have a tough conversation with their kids and put everything down in writing. Adult kids tend not to find my site, as they don't necessarily feel that they need any help making the situation work. It seems in some cases parents are really struggling and the kids are just not aware of this at all. This is compounded by parents not knowing how to express their concerns to their kids without sounding as though they are over-parenting.

I have had a few negative comments from younger people on some of my YouTube videos. They tend to say things such as, "You just don't understand how hard things are for young people these days," or, "You're awful for telling parents not to support their kids." This is interesting, because the focus of my materials is to help parents and adult kids live successfully together, with a plan that helps the adult child work toward independence. I discourage parents from having their kids live at home only if there are major conflict issues like violence, theft, or addiction issues the parent is not equipped to deal with, or if having the adult child living at home will put them in a nonviable financial position.

Q: *Do you think adult children living at home will be a more-or-less permanent feature of families going forward, or is this just a blip caused by the bad economy?*

A: I don't think this is a temporary blip. I launched my site in November 2007 – before the major economic issues – and it was already a growing trend at that time. I boomeranged for the first time in 2000, and most of my friends, and my parents' friends' kids, were doing it, too. I think returning home after university for six months to two years, rather than launching a career straight after graduation, is a trend that is here to stay. The return of older adult kids to the nest will likely be less of an issue as the economy improves, but this will not go away entirely, either.

Adult kids sometimes return to the nest for reasons that are not purely financial, especially after the end of a relationship or "starter marriage," when there are some major life issues to sort out. This is the situation I found myself in at 29 – I had a good job and could certainly pay my own bills, but I needed a home base for a while to sort out what direction my life was going to take next. The emotional support provided by parents is something young people today rely on much more than in previous generations.

They may be relying on it, but not without some discomfort. Just as there are websites to dispense advice to boomers who are still parenting, so are there outlets, including support groups on Facebook, where those on the receiving end may let everyone know how they feel.

It's hardly surprising, of course, that the put-upon millennials would have their own point of view – not that it's stopping them from living with their parents or accepting the financial help. But it would be inaccurate to say that the millennials only want to take the money. Increasingly, they are taking advice.

Re-education

This leads us to a third area in which the boomers are helping their children and grandchildren. The millennials are also becoming the object of programs that try to undo the deficiencies of their education and give them more practical (and especially job-related) skills. Apprenticeship programs, mentoring programs, financial literacy programs, intergenerational transfers of wisdom and experience – there are examples of these across North America.

Some of these programs have been created by colleges that were already in the "real world skills" business and have always had excellent networks of professionals who could teach or mentor on a part-time basis. Other programs have been created or sponsored by business organizations. Collectively, they demonstrate an important component of the boomers' never-ending interest in being active, engaged, and relevant – this time, by passing on their experience, skills, and insights to a younger generation that badly needs them.

Of course, the idea of experienced businessmen mentoring up-and-coming kids is not a new one. Junior Achievement, for example, works with elementary and high school students to educate them about "workforce readiness, entrepreneurship and financial literacy." Founded in the USA in 1916, Junior Achievement is a worldwide organization, operating in 123 countries. It now claims to reach 9.8 million students per year in over 400,000 classrooms and after-school locations. The programs, which include having the students start and run actual businesses, are taught by volunteers, many of whom are retirees with business experience.

Junior Achievement in Canada has reached over 2.7 million students in its 55-year history. In 2010, the organization ran programs in more than 400 communities, involving 13,000 volunteers and reaching more than 216,000 students.

One Junior Achievement graduate is William Meloche, who participated back in his high school days in the 1960s in Windsor, Ontario. He then went on to found a hugely successful advertising agency, sold it, and began a second career as a speaker, author, consultant, and investor.

Some of his activities have involved mentoring younger generations. Recently he set up the program The Business Studio, to bring celebrated business leaders to an audience of students for question-and-answer sessions captured on video and used in follow-on programs with larger audiences. A pilot program featured Isadore Sharp, founder and CEO of the Four Seasons Hotels chain; upcoming programs are being scheduled with other prominent business leaders.

I contacted Bill (I've been fortunate enough to work with him on some other projects) for information about how the program is working and what he is seeing among the millennials today and how he thinks things will play out.

He told me his program has been received very positively by business leaders and by academic institutions eager to be a venue for future programs. The businesses feel they can make an important contribution toward getting the students more equipped to deal with "real world" issues, and the academic institutions are starting to realize that their current programs may not plug into the real world sufficiently: Even MBA programs are under increased critical scrutiny for their relevance in today's workplace. There is a growing recognition that the voices of experience may be as useful as – or more useful than – the wisdom of tenured academics.

The idea of an intergenerational transfer of knowledge is, of course, as old as human history. Most tribal cultures have rituals and traditions associated with the receiving of advice from the elders. There are famous written records, too. We can go back more than 4,000 years to ancient Egypt and read the teachings of a Pharaoh (his exact identity is in scholarly dispute) written for his son Merika-re. ("Do not distinguish the son of a man of rank from a commoner, but take a man to yourself because of his actions.") We can study Lord Chesterfield's letters to his son *On the Fine Art of Becoming a Man of the World and a Gentleman*. The earl may have been an 18th-century version of a helicopter parent, because he unburdened himself of more than 400 missives, from 1746 to 1771. They included such famous instructions as, "Be wiser than other people if you can, but do not tell them so" and "Aim at perfection in everything, though in most things it is unattainable." (Alas, there is no evidence that the son, who predeceased his father, ever came close to measuring up.)

Three things, however, are different about what's happening now.

1. The scope and scale of that wisdom transfer and the

degree to which it is starting to get organized and systematized (and, yes, the Internet is playing a big role).

2. The fact that the dispensers of the wisdom are still, in a sense, competing with (or at least, very much sharing the stage with) their younger audience – *and expect to keep doing so for a meaningful period of time.*

3. The fact that dispensing wisdom is increasingly seen as a *benefit to the teachers* – i.e., that it reinforces their need to stay active and relevant, which is a need borne of their increased longevity as well as their unwillingness to *ever* give up that combination of "I matter" and "can do" that has been such a defining characteristic of their generation.

Mentoring has become a particularly strong trend in the area of entrepreneurship and start-ups. A good example is SCORE, a volunteer group in the USA that offers mentoring for entrepreneurs. There are over 13,000 mentors in the program, covering over 500 skills. SCORE helped more than 400,000 people in 2010 – almost a third more than in 2006. Interestingly, SCORE can deliver mentoring not just face to face but also online.

The mentors, of course, pick up interesting insights into the strengths and weaknesses of the learners. I asked Bill Meloche whether he was seeing anything in the young people he was mentoring and encountering through The Business Studio that reinforced any of my observations about the weaknesses of the millennials. Granted, by definition the population of millennials he was encountering were the most entrepreneurial and the most interested in acquiring practical skills. Even so, were they bringing anything to the party – either in their background and training or their attitudes – that could be a cause for concern?

Yes, he said, in an e-mail q&a. For one thing, their education was very light (not their fault) on entrepreneurial skills.

As a successful entrepreneur I was often amazed that brilliant students with much more cognitive capability than me, would find my views to be groundbreaking - when I had never taken part in formal business education myself. I had developed my own business instincts more as a Junior Achiever in high school (gaining practical experience) than through my post secondary education. Yet later I went on to build a very successful business.

I have mentioned this to other entrepreneurs (many of whom had built multi-million- or even multi-billion-dollar enterprises) who noticed the same thing. Some of the practices we found to be fundamental were not in the playbook of high-level business students. For example, you will never find anything on selling in an MBA program. Most MBA students and even their teachers would see that as beneath their level of expertise. In their minds selling is for someone else to do in the organization - not the leader. Yet most entrepreneurs require that capability to have any chance of building a business.

Next-generation business leaders must learn from people who have actually done it - because they do not get all they need to know in formal education. I developed The Business Studio to create an environment in which that can happen.

A second thing he noticed was that the entitlement germ was in evidence - even in this subset of the most competent, highly motivated, business-oriented millennials.

It's a combination of a sense of entitlement and being so used to having their needs taken care of that they expect this to happen even when they are starting a new business. Example: Young geniuses who start businesses have come to expect that investment bankers, venture capitalists, or angels will provide them with enough capital to cover their burn rate. If they run out, they can just go through another round of financing – after all, it's not their money. It would not occur to most of these budding entrepreneurs that they could go out and sell something or create a big groundbreaking deal themselves to cover their burn rate while they grow the business – and not have to depend on others to generate cash flow.

To be fair, there is growing evidence that many millennials are realizing the need to make themselves more job-market-ready. There is a steep growth, for example, in the number of those enrolling at community colleges who already have a university degree and are now seeking more specialized training. The *Globe and Mail* reported on this trend in a May 2011 article by Tralee Pearce, "Job-Seeking University Graduates Give It the Old College Try."

As the bachelor's degree loses its lustre, the college system has been prepping for its close-up. One of its biggest boosters: university graduates who are treating colleges and polytechnics as de facto finishing schools. "Our biggest area of growth is post-university students," said James Knight, the president of the Association of Canadian Community Colleges.

The article goes on to give some examples. At Humber College in Toronto, 31% of incoming students the previous fall already had a degree or other postsecondary studies. At the BC Institute of Technology, 20% of incoming students already held undergrad degrees, and a further 30% already had some post-secondary education.

So it's certainly not accurate to say that the millennials are all waiting for the boomers to extend a helping hand and are doing little or nothing on their own. Nevertheless, boomer help – with money, with housing, with counsel – not only can be decisive, but also can alleviate some of the intergenerational friction that we are witnessing. Anya Kamenetz, author of *Generation Debt*, agrees.

> *I do see signs of this intergenerational transfer of knowledge and care, and I think it's really important. Not only will Boomers have to share with their children, but many Millennials are finding it necessary to take care of and share resources with Mom and Dad.*

On the other hand, she's sceptical about my thesis: "Ultimately, the real battle is not between generations. It's between the rich and the poor." (Which calls for a whole other book, of course – but cheer up, a whole library on that topic is already being produced.)

As mentioned earlier, Anya Kamenetz characterizes the millennials as Generation Debt, and my friend and colleague Brent Green characterizes the boomers as Generation Reinvention. Brent supported my sense that the Age Rage war will come to some kind of a Marshall Plan resolution, but went a lot further. He had this to say in an e-mail exchange:

> *Boomers are worried about the fate of their children as much as any generation worries that offspring will have optimum chances for success and well-being. Many boomer parents are actively deferring and modifying their needs to accommodate extended financial and emotional dependence of their grown children. Retirement plans are being adapted; financial support is being provided. Some of the choices being made by young people to return home – and their boomer parents providing them sanctuary – can be attributed to the recessionary economy of the last several years.*

But another view is being proffered, Brent said, by Jeffrey Arnett, a psychology professor at Clark University. Arnett believes a new life stage has become manifest with the youngest generations today; he calls it "emerging adulthood."

According to Arnett, Brent told me, "20-somethings today are forestalling some of the developmental hurdles associated with full adulthood, including establishing lifelong career commitments, gaining true financial independence, and committing to marriage and parenting." This is supported by some of the statistics we have already noted, and Brent provided additional confirmation.

Nearly 30% of parents have been compelled to refinance their homes to help support their adult children beyond the college years. Additionally, two-thirds of parents confronted by longer-term support for a boomerang child must reduce daily living costs and other expenses in order to pay for a child's added living expenses burden. One-third of baby boomers who have assisted adult children must then address a reduction to retirement savings. These financial realities come with the greater acceptance among millennials to move home with parents after college graduation. One study reported that 85% of today's college graduates plan to move home for a transition period of at least a few months' duration between college and full career adaptation. Given a poor job climate and extraordinary college loan debt, many millennials may return home not for just months but for several years.

"This 21st century form of dependence between adult millennials and their boomer parents suggests changing dynamics in the parent-child interpersonal relationship," Brent went on to say.

> *One Pew study found that millennials aren't as rebellious as their boomer parents were back in the 1960s and 1970s. Boomers invested a great deal of emotional energy and social disruption rebelling against the values of their parents, the GI generation; millennials, on the other hand, have demonstrated greater tolerance of their boomer parents' values. Some embrace their parents today as friends rather than adversaries or authority*

figures fomenting harsh dismissal. Although the future dynamics between old-old boomers and their middle-aged millennial is speculative, some sociologists believe it's reasonable to predict that children in their 20s who have received extra parental assistance and life coaching from parents may be predisposed to recompense their parents when eventually the parents need financial assistance.

If so, it may be out of guilt feelings. Brent notes that "millennial children who became boomerang young adults may also carry the a measure of guilt with knowledge that their extended 'emerging adulthood' limited their parents' ability to save adequately for a long retirement. Whether millennials are driven by guilt or a welcome sense of familial duty, it's reasonable that intergenerational bonds will strengthen as the youngest generation matures into full adulthood."

Brent's observations indicate that a much more profound and long-lasting set of dynamics is at work here – the creation of emerging adulthood as a new life-stage category, which in turn triggers a fundamental rethinking of the traditional roles of parent and child.

Brent also points out, fairly, that some of the characteristics of emerging adulthood – focusing on change, not settling down – were attached to the boomers themselves by a Yale professor in 1970. But if the boomers were not quickly settling down to the same Pleasantville lifestyle as their parents, they were at least more independent and self-reliant than the millennials. As we have seen, for example, the boomer rate of continuing to live at home after university was *less than half* the rate of today.

If parent-child roles are being reinvented – which is the logical flip side of the way boomers are reinventing aging – can we identify some structures or organizations that are leading the way? We've already seen one simple manifestation – books and websites, such as Christina Newberry's, on how to manage adult children. Is there anything wider-ranging?

Brent pointed me to Generations United (gu.org), an organization that encourages intergenerational dialogue and cooperation.

www.gu.org/

This organization completed an important research study in September 2011, *Family Matters: Multigenerational Families in a Volatile Economy*. The study, conducted by Harris Interactive, polled over 2,000 US residents ages 18 and up. One in six reported living in a multigenerational household and pointed to the tough economy as the major reason.

- 21% of those living in a multigenerational household said the economy was the only factor; 66% said it was one factor among others
- 40% reported that a job loss, change in job status, or underemployment a reason the family became a multigenerational household
- 20% said health-care costs were a factor
- 14% said foreclosure or other loss of housing was the reason

An overwhelming majority reported that they had benefited from the new arrangements. For example, 72% said the financial situation of at least one family member had improved. And 52% reported that the new arrangements had made it possible for a family member to continue school or job training. Not surprisingly, 82% thought there should be more government programs and policies to support multigenerational households.

But it was more than dollars and cents. For example, 82% said the arrangement "enhanced bonds or relationships among family members," while 75% said the arrangement made it "easier to provide for care needs" such as child care or older adult care. On the other hand, 78% reported that "at times, my family's multigenerational arrangements can contribute to stress among family members."

The organization has put forward a number of innovative policy recommendations to national and local governments. These include better housing programs (from changes in building codes to make it easier to renovate or adapt housing for multigenerational accommodation, to financial support for housing modification) and better support for caregivers. It has also put forth some recommendations for employers, including more flexible family leave policies and changes to employee benefit programs to make them more accommodating to multigenerational families.

The number of multigenerational families in the USA has increased by 30% since 2000, according to the US Census Bureau, and homebuilders have responded with designs that specifically address their needs. Forget the retrofitted "granny flat" – we're talking about a new style of home that takes into account the presence of a grandparent or adult child, with a separate suite, including bathroom, integrated into the overall design of the home. "This is a niche area that appears to be solid and growing," said Stephen Melman, director of economic services at the National Association of Home Builders, in a telephone interview reported on Bloomberg.com on November 16, 2011.

The same trend is being observed in Canada. "The Multi-generational Home Makes a Comeback" was the headline of a *Globe and Mail* story by Sydney Loney, on January 20, 2011. Loney observes: "Whether it's boomerang children returning home or retirees angling for more face time with the grand-kids, an increasing number of Canadians are choosing to reside in multi-generational family groups. And both builders and municipalities are taking note, with flexible housing options and a loosening of zoning restrictions."

The article quotes Susan Newman, author of *Under One Roof Again: All Grown Up and (Re)learning to Live Together Happily*: "People are realizing that family members are the first line of support when someone needs help." It goes on to note that "what often begins as a short-term stay evolves into a long-term living arrangement. Many families find the pros of shared accommodation (reduced expenses, close proximity to aging family members and built-in babysitting) outweigh the cons (occasional friction and finding oneself in a queue for the bathroom)."

As in the USA, Canadian homebuilders are responding. The article mentions Metric Homes, in Ottawa, which, thanks to new zoning bylaws, is starting to market a home-within-a-home. "From the street, the dwellings look like single-family homes, but behind the exterior walls are two buildings: a two-storey house with a bungalow attached."

Intrigued, I went to the Metric Homes website and found this more detailed description:

> *From the outside it looks like a large single family home so it fits with the family home subdivision profile that it's built amongst, but really it is two completely separate dwellings with their own private entrances plus common areas between them. Each home also has its*

own electrical, water and heating system allowing for two family groups to live independently of each other. There's also fireproofing between each home for added security.

The website also lays out a rationale for the concept – one that plays perfectly into the underlying social trends that we have been describing.

By pooling resources with the older generation, adult children and their families can live in a neighbourhood that may be beyond their reach otherwise. Backyard facilities (e.g., decks, pools) can also be shared from a cost and maintenance perspective. The older generation may not want to live in an "adult lifestyle" community and can continue to live in a regular neighbourhood with help on hand with the yard that perhaps they can't or don't want to maintain anymore. By contracting help a nursing home could be avoided altogether. Grandparents see more of their grandchildren. Also parents wishing to travel have the added security of not leaving their home empty for weeks or even months at a time.

Canadian home design firm Drummond House Plans offers building plans to suit a variety of financial and lifestyle needs. "With the greater life span of the population and young adult children going back home to save money while getting their careers moving forward, the category of bi-generational or intergenerational houses has become a 21st century trend," their website says in its introduction to a home plan collection for the multigenerational and extended family. "These Drummond house designs and house floor plans are defined as one structure with separate units. With generous layouts and four to five bedrooms, these Drummond houses are ideal for keeping family together without sacrificing independence." Over 20 plans are available.

We can certainly expect to see this trend in housing to

continue. Not only does this approach address the emerging multigenerational family trend, but it also has important follow-on benefits, particularly in terms of reducing long-term health-care costs. Independent living, or aging in place, is a hot topic now: The boomers want to retain their independence for as long as possible, and cash-strapped governments want to keep the elderly out of expensive long-term care facilities for as long as possible.

The multigenerational household – particularly if it can be located in an environment designed from the start to accommodate its needs (as opposed to the retrofitted "granny flat") – could represent an ideal solution: The younger caregivers (boomers for their senior parents, Gen Xers or millennials for their boomer parents) would now be living right on the spot, and the home can include a number of design and tech features that promote independent living (better accessibility, health and safety monitoring). It's a win-win all around – the family benefits, as does society, through lower health-care costs. Expect to see governments – particularly municipalities, whence come all those zoning bylaws and building codes – increase their support for multigenerational housing and services.

To sum up: It is clear that even while the boomers and seniors are not letting up in the aggressive pursuit of their own interests (jobs, pensions, health care), they are at the same time extending significant help to the struggling millennials. This help often requires some sacrifice, such as the postponement or rearrangement of retirement plans or the cashing in of home equity in order to downsize. Even so, the older generations are stepping up. The Marshall Plan is already operative, even if some intergenerational sniping continues.

Age Rage may be real enough when it comes to rhetoric; however, where substance is concerned, the boomers and seniors are definitely solving the war of the generations.

Conclusion

WILL Age Rage end? How? And if the boomers and seniors are actually taking care of things, if the war is more apparent than real, what will all the shouting and fist-shaking leave behind?

The boomers will not, as a generation, suddenly decide to ease up in their determination to fulfill their needs and wants to stay powerful and relevant, to stay engaged, to have enough money to sustain a much longer life span, to collect every possible dime of pension entitlements, to preserve every possible dime of health-care spending from which they might benefit. The boomers will get all, or most, of what they are after.

The millennials will not, as a generation, suddenly decide to stop criticizing the boomers. They will not suddenly decide to stop feeling angry about the bad hand they have been dealt – particularly if that bad hand requires them to pay higher taxes on lower earnings for no other reason than to clean up the debt mess they have inherited. Neither will the millennials quickly overcome the deficiencies they have been left with as a result of the social, cultural and, above all, educational environment in which they have grown up.

The war will linger, if only in metaphor, and then gradually peter out, acquiring some of the attributes of real physical wars of the past – memoirs, persistent feuds, symbols, and tropes.

If we stopped with that observation (and I don't think my prediction is terribly risky), we might miss a more interesting, and even constructive, aspect of Age Rage.

Age Rage was not merely an undesirable by-product of certain dynamics that could have been avoided or better handled. Age Rage was always inevitable: We were never going to be able to add three or four decades to the human life span (with even more to come, if we believe certain scientists) without at some point undergoing a shock treatment that would compel us to realize just how big the implications were ... and to motivate us to respond forcefully.

In a way, Age Rage could be seen as that catalyst.

Age Rage was a way of holding our feet to the fire, forcing us to more urgently address the necessary (and big) questions – how the older generations can better prepare the younger; what generations owe to each other (and new ways, perhaps, that they can help each other); how society can and should allocate increasingly scarce resources; how public policy should be adjusted to respond sooner to inexorable demographic and attitudinal trends, so as to avoid sudden shocks or squeeze plays where there isn't enough time or money to alleviate serious problems.

By its very intensity, the phenomenon of Age Rage drove us to grapple with these issues to better understand their long-term implications. Given the breathtaking scale of these implications, Age Rage should have come as no surprise: *Of course* we flailed; *of course* we berated and bemoaned and accused and were afraid. We were finally beginning to understand – we are *still* only beginning to understand – the reinvention of aging not just as an interesting individual or even group phenomenon, but as a staggering revolution requiring changes to virtually every social attitude and institution.

The reinvention of aging, after all, also implies the reinvention of youth.

How could we have expected that process to be carried out gently and tidily and with no noise?

There is a dual identity, for both sets of protagonists, that makes the process even more intense. The boomers and seniors, on one side, and the millennials, on the other, are simultaneously the last generations of the old model and the first generations of the new. Each is coping with expectations from the past, while at the same time foreshadowing the norms of the future.

"Look at those greedy boomers, hanging on and refusing to get out of the way" is a sentiment that is possible only because of the norms of the past, when people *were* expected to get out of the way at a certain age. In a future world, the norm will be to keep working, possibly for decades longer than today.

"Look at those infantile millennials, incapable of coping" is a sentiment that is possible only because of the norms of the past, when people *were* expected to already be adults at a certain age. In a future world, where life spans may top 100, the norm may be to arrive at adulthood at 30 or later. After all, in percentage terms, this would represent the same degree along the life span – somewhere between a quarter and a third – as adulthood in one's young 20s would represent today.

It should not be surprising that the transition from the old norms to the emerging new norms is difficult and acrimonious.

The process could never have been anything but rowdy.

Age Rage was always going to come.

Its intensity will fade as the two armies shed more of their past identities (and the accompanying norms and expectations) and take on more of their future ones. When that process is complete, Age Rage will have morphed, especially for the millennials, into a kind of retroactive positive experience. The millennials will remember it the way the parents and grandparents of the boomers remembered the Depression, finding (but not until years later) all kinds of redeeming benefits in the despair they felt at the time. They'll revel in the wounds they suffered; they'll scratch at the scar tissue and say to their children, "You should have seen how hard it was, but we got through it."

And then they'll carry a tray of food upstairs to their 110-year-old boomer parent, who will be playing Sudoku (to keep the brain sharp) on a tablet while fielding "Remember-when" e-mails from friends invoking the *Leave It to Beaver* days when you could ride a bike and not have to wear a helmet.

A Note on Sources

FOR the convenience of the reader, I have indicated my sources – particularly in the case of books, articles, and blogs – directly in the text. The references below cover the sources of statistics cited throughout the book. In some cases, I relied on a single source; in others, I compiled or created an exhibit from a number of sources.

Chapter 1 – This Time, It's Different

I worked with several sources regarding (a) the percentage distribution of population by age and (b) projections of future distribution of population by age. Both Statistics Canada <www.statcan.gc.ca> and the US Census Bureau <www.census.gov/> present data covering different permutations and combinations of age groups and date ranges. I also consulted the National Institute on Aging <www.nia.nih.gov/>, a branch of the US Department of Health and Human Services.

Chapter 2 – The Converging Causes

Data on life expectancy at birth are from Statistics Canada <www40.statcan.gc.ca/l01/cst01/health26-eng.

htm>. Statistics Canada is also the source of the Canadian population pyramid, which it presents in animated form at <www.statcan.gc.ca/ads-annonces/91-520-x/pyra-eng.htm>. US data are from the US Census Bureau <www.census.gov/population/www/projections/natchart.html>.

I drew on several tables from Statistics Canada to construct the comparisons of population, by age group, during the Great Depression and today.

Chapter 3 – Boomers and Seniors: Firepower

The *ZOOMER* magazine online media kit – and media kits for the other ZoomerMedia properties – may be found at <www.zoomermedia.ca/>.

Statistics about market size and spending power were compiled from a number of sources, including ZoomerMedia sales presentations, and, in the case of US data, Nancy Padberg at Navigate Boomer Media <www.navigateboomermedia.com> and Mary Furlong & Associates <www.maryfurlong.com>.

Chapter 5 – Boomers and Seniors: Objectives

I consulted a number of studies about health-care spending in Canada and the USA, including: the Fraser Institute's report "Canada's Medicare Bubble" <www.ledevoir.com/documents/pdf/medicare_bubble.pdf>; a comparative study by the Organisation for Economic Co-operation and Development (OECD) <www.oecd.org/dataoecd/46/33/38979719.pdf>; and a US Congressional research study comparing US spending with that of other OECD countries <http://assets.opencrs.com/rpts/RL34175_20070917.pdf>.

The 2011 report of the trustees of the US Social Security system may be found at <www.ssa.gov/oact/tr/2011/tr2011.pdf>.

Chapter 6 – Millennials: The Kids Are Not All Right

The graph on fertility rates was compiled from Statistics Canada <www.statscan.gc.ca> and the National Center for Health Statistics <www.cdc.gov/nchs/>.

Chapter 7 – The Jobs Batttle

Data on employment rates and participation rates, by age group, are from Statistics Canada <www.statscan.gc.ca> and the US Bureau of Labor Statistics <www.bls.gov>.
The chart on changes in the US participation rate comes from Wells Fargo Bank, as reported in an article at <static5.businessinsider.com/image/4e6bfea269b eddb828000003-604-445/unemployment.jpg>.

Chapter 8 – The Political Battle

Data on the age distribution of voters and voter turnout in Canada and the USA are a composite of data from Elections Canada <www.elections.ca> and the US Census Bureau <www.census.gov>.

Index

AARP (American Association of Retired Persons), 104–105, 129, 137, 141, 142, 157, 165
Adams, Michael, 48
Adbusters, 154–155, 156, 159, 163, 165
age rage
 five causes of, 10, 22–23
aging in place, 29, 44, 193, 194
AllBusiness.com, 105
American Interest, The, 96
American Seniors Association, 129
American Spectator, 60
AnswersYahoo.com, 112
Arnett, Jeffrey, 187, 188
Association of Canadian Community Colleges, 186
Atlantic, The, 72, 114, 115, 169, 171

baby boomers. *See* boomers
Baker, Russell, 65–67
Baruch College of Public Affairs, 145
Bass, David N., 60
Battle Hymn of the Tiger Mother (Chua), 69
BC Institute of Technology, 186
Beckett, Francis, 38
Begala, Paul, 37, 38, 39, 41
Better Homes and Gardens, 174
Bevis, Jeff, 106
birth control pill, 64, 65
Bloomberg.com, 192
BMO Retirement Institute, 106
boomerang children, 176, 188, 189, 192
 See also boomers: sharing homes with adult children; millennials: living with parents; multigenerational households

203

Boomer Group, 111
BoomerPreneurs, 106–107, 110
boomers
   adaptability of, 41–44, 104
   assisting parents, 43, 173, 194
   birth control and, 64–66
   child-rearing vaues of, 63, 68, 74
      See also helicopter parents
   consumers, as, 30–31
   debt and, 49, 61, 68, 85, 170, 195
   definition of, xiii
   economic anxieties/fears of, 47–48, 56–57
   entrepreneurs, as, 106
   financially assisting children/grandchildren, 43, 99, 113, 118, 119, 173, 174, 176, 187, 194
   health-care and, 43–44, 51, 52, 56, 57, 122
   Internet and, 31, 32, 33, 44, 101
   job experience skills of, 95, 111
   job-finding networks/industry for, 101, 103, 109
   life stages (as compared with Gen X and millennials), 175–176
   marketing to, 27–31
   mentoring by, 182, 183, 184, 187
   more self-reliant than millennials, as, 189
   music of, 37–38, 41
   pensions and, 19, 36, 48–50, 57, 83, 122, 194
   percentage of population, as (with seniors), 14, 15
   perceived selfishness/greed of, 6, 37–40, 99, 100, 113, 114–115, 116, 117, 118, 119, 136–137, 167, 169, 197
   political affiliation of, 126–128
   positive innovations of, 37, 41
   power of, 28, 29, 34, 38, 65, 66–67
   rebelling against parents, 188
   reinventing aging, 5, 19, 62, 84, 104, 169, 189
   reinventing parenting, 169
   retirement, deferment of, 7, 19, 20, 22, 41, 83–86, 87–88, 92–95, 99, 100, 105, 167, 176, 187
   retirement underfunding of, 19, 41, 48, 49, 57, 83, 84, 85, 92–93, 98, 100, 105, 188, 189
   savings of, 48–50, 84
   self-employment and, 106, 109
   self-loathing and, 169, 171
   sharing homes with adult children, 175, 176–181, 187, 191–194
   stress and, 176
   supporting parents, 57, 113
   temp employees, as, 109, 111
   unemployment and, 90, 91, 92, 103
   voting power of (with seniors), 20, 124, 125, 157, 167
Boston's National Public Radio affiliate website, 93
Boyd, Suzanne, 27

British Columbia Securities Commission (BCSC), 71
Bureau of Labor Statistics, 95
Business Studio,The, 182, 183, 184, 185
BusinessInsider.com, 93

Cain, Herman, 152
Campus Confidential: 100 Startling Things You Didn't Know About Canadian Universities (Coates, Morrison), 59
Canada Pension Plan (CPP), 36, 133
Canadian Federation of Students, 137, 139, 140
career fairs for older workers, 104
Career Rookie, 101
CareerBuilder Canada, 108
CARP, 129–131, 132, 134, 135, 136, 137, 138, 140, 141, 142
centenarians, 4, 47
Chamberlain, Lisa, 171–172
Chesterfield, Lord, 183
Chevreau, Jonathan, 109, 176
Chretien, Jean, 134
Chrysler, 96
Chua, Amy, 69
civil rights, 41, 158, 159, 161–163
Clark University, 187
Clinton, Bill, 37
CNN Money, 95
Coates, Ken, 59, 60, 74, 75–78, 80
community colleges, 78, 79
Conservative Party, 18, 36, 126, 127, 128, 132, 134
  See also Harper government
Conte, Victoria, 105
Cravit, Cynthia Ross, 108

Daily Mail, 38
debt, 16–17, 39, 49, 61, 68, 74, 78, 79, 80, 85, 100, 122, 141, 148, 167, 170, 187, 188, 195
DeLong, David, 109
Democratic Party, 161, 163
Dr. Sears, 69
Drummond House Plans, 193

echo boomers. *See* millennials
e-commerce, 31, 32
economic meltdown. *See* financial crisis
Economist, The, 79
education funding, 6, 7, 51, 83, 120, 139, 140, 141, 167
education bubble, 78–79
Ego Boom: Why the World Really Does Revolve Around You, The, (George, Maich), 97
EKOS Research, 127
Elections Canada, 124, 201
Elementary Teachers Federation of Ontario (EFTO), 139

emerging adulthood, 187, 189
Eng, Susan, 130, 131, 134, 136, 140
entitlement generation. *See* millennials
estate tax, 170, 171, 172
    See also taxes
Ewing Marion Kauffman Foundation, 105

Facebook, 33, 152, 181
Family Matters: Multigenerational Families in a Volatile Economy (Generations United), 190
FastCompany.com, 145
fertility, 64–65
financial crisis, x, 18, 22, 47, 48, 62, 72, 84, 85, 86, 88, 92, 97, 167, 173, 180
financial crisis in Europe, 16, 136
Financial Post, 99, 176
First Light Home Care, 106
Flaherty, Jim, 134
Fonda, Jane, 164
Forbes magazine, 174
Fortune magazine, 59
Forum Research, 176
Four Seasons Hotels, 182
Fraser Institute, 200
Free Republic, 39
Furlong, Mary, 29

Gallup polls, 126
General Motors, 97
Generation Debt: Why Now Is a Terrible Time to Be Young (Kamenetz), 61, 78, 79, 187
Generation Me. *See* millennials
Generation Reinvention, 28, 42, 187
Generation X, xiv, 39, 71, 74, 88, 99, 124, 125, 172, 173, 174, 175–176, 194
Generation Y. *See* millennials
Generations United, 190, 191
George, Lianne, 97–98
Globe and Mail, The, 134, 135, 186, 192
Goar, Carol, 99
Google, 38, 69
government funding squeeze, 51, 83–84, 120–123, 141, 167
grade inflation, 68, 74, 76
Gramsci, Antonio, 162
Graves, Frank, 127, 128
Great Depression, xiv, 17–19, 198, 200
Greatest Generation, 169, 170
Green, Brent, 28, 42–43, 187, 188, 189
Guaranteed Income Supplement (GIS), 131, 132
Guardian, The, 38

Hands-on Guide to Surviving Adult Children Living at Home, The (Newberry), 177

Hanson, Maria, 95
Harper, Stephen, 127, 128, 132, 133, 134, 136
Harper, Tim, 127
Harper government, 36, 135
    See also Conservative Party
Harris Interactive, 190
Hayden, Tom, 160–164
Health Canada, 53
health care, 6, 8, 16, 20, 21, 31, 41, 43, 44, 50–56, 83, 122, 133, 167, 194, 195
helicopter parents, 68, 69, 74, 183
    See also boomers: child-rearing values of
Hesiod, 3, 72
hippies, 70, 116, 164
home equity, cashing in of,194
Howe, Neil, 58, 73–74
Humber College, 186

independent living. See aging in place
Intern Nation: How to Earn Nothing and Learn Little in the Brave New Economy
    (Perlin), 101
intergenerational houses
    See multigenerational households
International Mature Marketing Network, 28
Internet, 16, 27, 31–33, 44, 97, 101, 104, 177, 184
internships, unpaid, 101–102
Investors Group, 173

job clearing house, 110
job-finding institutions, 101
job-finding networks, 103
job networking websites, 109, 110
jobs, competition for, 62, 83, 86, 88, 91–95, 98–100, 101, 102, 167
Johnson, Lyndon, 163
Junior Achievement, 182

Kahn, Lisa, 73
Kamenetz, Anya, 61, 78–79, 187
Kinsley, Michael, 169–172
Klein, Stephanie, 111
Knight, James, 186
knowledge retention, 110
knowledge transfer. See boomers: mentoring by
Koff, Art, 105
Kremer, Amy, 152

labor force, demographics of, 85, 86, 89, 94
Lancaster, Lynne C., 88, 89
Lancaster University Management School, 95
Layton, Jack, 127, 128
League for Industrial Democracy, 159
Lehman Brothers, 73

Liberal Party, 18, 35, 128, 132, 133, 134, 139, 141
life span, x, 4, 5, 6, 10, 37, 44, 52, 166, 193, 195, 196, 197
  See also longevity
LinkedIn, 101
lobby groups, 121, 167
Loney, Sydney, 192
longevity, 4, 8, 9, 10, 15, 22, 36, 43, 47, 48, 49, 84, 93, 166, 184
  See also life span
Lost Knowledge: Confronting the Threat of an Aging Workforce (DeLong), 109
Lovett-Reid, Patricia, 106
Lu, Vanessa, 99
Lugar, Richard, 152

Mackenzie King, William Lyon, 35
Maclean's magazine, 97
Marshall Plan, 7, 168, 187, 194
Mary Furlong & Associates, 200
Matchpoint Franchise Consulting Network, 105
McDonald's, 42, 95, 98
Me Generation. *See* boomers
Mead, Walter Russell, 96, 97, 116
median age, 128
Medicaid, 54
Medicare, 55–56
Melman, Stephen, 191
Meloche, William, 182, 183, 184–186
Merike-re, 183
Metric Homes, 192–193
MetropolitanToronto Police Services Board, 130
Millennial Pendulum, The (New America Foundation), 126
millennials
  academic unpreparedness and, 59–60, 70, 74, 75–76
  caregivers of parents, as,194
  definition of, xiv
  delayed parenthood and, 61, 99
  entitlement generation, as, 58–61, 75, 76, 97, 115, 139, 168, 173, 185
  entrepreneurial skills, lacking, 184
  extended adolescence/infantilism of, 60–61, 69, 70, 116, 157, 188, 197
  financial expectations of, 72
  home ownership and, 72
  inflated grades and, 154
  inherited debt and, 61–62, 100, 195
  Internet savvy of, 97, 101
  life stages of, compared with boomers and Gen X, 175–176
  living with parents, 174–181, 188
  optimism of, 71, 72, 73
  political affiliation of, 126–127
  re-education and, 186
  savings of, 50
  self-esteem issues of, 58, 61, 69, 78, 80, 97–98, 109, 154, 156

self-reliance, lacking (compared to boomers), 189
social media and, 32, 101
spoiled whiners, perceived as, 58, 168
student debt and, 61, 78, 80, 100, 122, 167, 188
tolerant of parents' values vs boomers, 188–189
trophy kids, as, 74
unemployment and, 89–94, 99
unrealistic wage expectations of, 71–72, 97
votes cast by, 124, 125
work expectations of, 59, 61, 97
work ethic, lacking of, 61, 168
Millennials: A Portrait of Generation Next (Pew Research Center), 71
Millennials Rising (Howe), 73
MIT AgeLab, 109
Morrison, Bill, 59
Morris, Michael, 109, 110
MSNMoney.com, 106
Mulroney, Brian, 134
multigenerational households
  aging in place and, 193, 194
  benefits of, 191, 192, 193, 194
  better housing programs for, 191, 192, 194
  new style of homes for, 191
  reasons given for, 190, 193
  See also boomers: sharing homes with adult children; millennials: living with parents

National Association of Home Builders, 191
National Center for Health Statistics, 201
National Institute on Aging, 199
National Endowment for Financial Education, 174
National Post, 109, 136
National Report Card on Youth Financial Literacy (BCSC), 71
Navigate Boomer Media, 28, 200
Nelson, Ben, 152
Net Gen. *See* millennials
New America Foundation, 126
New Democratic Party (NDP), 128, 132
New Old, The (Cravit), ix, x, 5, 19, 28, 37
New York Times, 58, 65, 96, 97, 111
Newberry, Christina, 179–181, 189
Newman, Susan, 192
Northeastern University, 95

Obama, Barack, 129
Obamacare, 129, 147
Oborne, Peter, 38–39
Occupy movement, 142, 143, 144, 145, 146, 147, 153, 154, 157, 158, 160, 163
Occupy Toronto, 150–152
Occupy Wall Street, 73, 143, 147, 148–150

Old Age Pension (1927), 35
Old Age Security (OAS) program, 132–137
online polling, 131
Ontario Coalition of Chinese Head Tax Payers and Families, 130–131
Organisation for Economic Co-operation and Development (OECD), 200

Padberg, Nancy, 28, 200
parent-child roles changing, 189
Peck, Don, 72–73
Perlin, Ross, 101–102
pensions. *See* boomers: pensions and; Canadian Pension Plan; Old Age Security
    program; Social Security; seniors: pensions and
Pearce, Tralee, 186
Pew Research Center, 71, 73, 188
Pinch, The, (Willetts), 38
political correctness, 68
polls, online, 131
population pyramid, 12–13
    See also life span; longevity
population replacement rate, 64–65
Port Huron Statement, 159, 160, 165

Rae, Bob, 133–134
recessionary economy, 71, 73, 85, 187
re-education, 181–182
re-entry to workforce. *See* seniors: re-entering work force
reinvention of aging, ix, x, 5, 7, 8, 19, 22, 62, 84, 104, 169, 189, 196
Republican Party, 146, 148, 150, 152
RetiredBrains.com, 105
retirement. *See* boomers: retirement, deferment of; seniors: retirement, deferment of
returning home
    See boomerang children; millennials: living with parents; multigenerational households
Ringer, Carol, 111
Russell, Deborah, 105

sandwich effect, 43
Schoen, Douglas, 145
School Administrator magazine, 73
Schwerner, Michael, 159
SCORE, 184
Sellers, Patricia, 59
seniors
    CARP and, 130, 131, 132, 134, 135, 136
    definition of, xiii–xiv
    financially assisting children/grandchildren, 173, 194
    franchises and, 105, 106
    Guaranteed Income Supplement (GIS) and, 131, 132
    health care and, 51, 52, 53, 57, 83, 96, 122, 167

Internet and, 31, 32, 101
job skills of, 106
marketing to, 27, 28, 29, 31
Old Age Security (OAS) and, 133, 135, 136
pensions and, 36, 48–50, 83, 122, 167
percentage of population, as (with boomers), 14, 15
pessimism of, 71
political affiliation of, 126–128
re-entering work force, 19, 20, 92–93, 95, 105, 110, 120, 167
retirement, deferment of, 20, 22, 84, 86, 87, 92–94, 194
retirement funds lacking of, 48, 83, 92, 95, 100, 105
savings and, 50
self-employment and, 105
temp employees, as, 109, 111
unemployment and, 87, 90–92, 93
voting power of (with boomers), 20, 124, 125, 157, 167
Sharp, Isadore, 182
Shufelt, Tim, 99–100
Silent Generation, the. *See* seniors
Slackonomics: Generation X in the Age of Creative Destruction (Chamberlain), 171
Snowe, Olympia, 152
social media, 32, 33, 102, 121, 129, 153
 See also Facebook; Twitter; YouTube
Social Security, 16, 49, 55, 56, 92, 114, 133, 157, 171, 200
socialstrategygroup.com, 109
Socrates, 3, 5
Souzen, Sherri, 39
Stabenow, Debby, 152
Stanhope, Philip Dormer. *See* Chesterfield, Lord
Statistics Canada, 10, 12, 14, 49, 67, 72, 84, 85, 86, 90, 174, 199, 200, 201
Stayin' Alive: How Canadian Baby Boomers Will Work, Play, and Find Meaning in the Second Half of Their Adult Lives (Adams), 48
Stillman, David, 88, 89
Strauss, William, 58
Students for a Democratic Society (SDS), 159–160
student loan debt, 61, 78, 79, 80, 83, 100, 122, 137, 167, 188
Sum, Andrew, 95
Swift, Jonathan, 3

taxes, 50, 51, 52, 55, 56, 96, 120, 121, 122, 195
TD Canada Trust, 176
Tea Party Express, 142, 143, 144, 145, 146, 147, 148, 150, 152, 153–154
TheTicker.com, 101
Thiel, Paul, 79–80
Toronto Star, 99, 127, 139
Total Fertility Rate (TFR), 64, 65, 67, 68
Trudeau, Pierre Elliott, 159
Trudeaumania, 158
Tseng, Nin-Hai, 95

tuition-rebate program, 139
Tuttle, Brad, 118
Twitter, 152
two-tier pay system, 96

Under One Roof Again: All Grown Up and (Re)learning to Live Together Happily (Newman), 192
unemployment, 72, 86, 87, 88, 90, 91, 100, 103, 104, 114, 201
United Auto Workers, 97
United States Students Association, 140–141
US Bureau of Labor Statistics, 201
US Census Bureau, 124, 191, 199, 200, 201
US Congress, 55, 148, 152, 160, 161, 162, 200
US Department of Health and Human Services, 199
US Department of Labor, 85
US Social Security. *See* Social Security
US Trust survey, 117

VibrantNation.com, 174
Vietnam War, 41, 116, 158, 159, 163
Volkswagen Beetle, 42
voter turnout, 5, 20, 125, 127, 128
votes cast by age group, 5, 20, 72, 124–125, 138, 157

Wall Street Journal, 97
Warner, Judith, 58
Waugh, Evelyn, 4
Weather Underground, 160, 164
Weisenthal, Joe, 93
Wells Fargo, 93, 100, 201
Wente, Margaret, 134, 135
When Generations Collide (Lancaster, Stillman), 88–89
Why-Worry generation. *See* millennials
Wilde, Oscar, 4
Willetts, David, 38
Winerip, Michael, 111
Winston Group, 144
World Economic Forum, 132
World War II, xiii, xiv, 11, 65, 170, 171
www.boomerscloud.com, 109

YouTube, 153, 180
Yuppies, 42, 70, 116, 164

Znaimer, Moses, 5, 27, 130, 131
ZOOMER magazine, 27, 130, 200
Zoomer Show, 130
ZoomerMedia Limited, xi, 27, 28, 130, 131, 200
Zoomers, 5, 138
  See also boomers; seniors

CPSIA information can be obtained at www.ICGtesting.com
Printed in the USA
LVOW082309050412

276383LV00005B/2/P